COASTAL
NAVIGATION
for
BEGINNERS

Jeff Toghill

Ward Lock Limited ● London

First published in Australia 1976
Reprinted 1978
Revised 1980
This edition first published in Great Britain in 1980 by Ward Lock Limited,
116 Baker Street, London W1M 2BB, A Pentos Company

ISBN 0-7063-5987-9

Set by ASA Typesestters, Sydney
Printed and bound by Everbest Printing Co Ltd, Hong Kong

Contents

Introduction

The success of my previous books *Manual of Yacht Navigation* and the more comprehensive *Yachtsman's Navigation Manual* brought home the remarkable interest of yachtsmen, both sail and power, in the subject of navigation. Both these books are simplified and adapted for yachts and small craft as opposed to the totally different and complex subject of 'big-ship' navigation, but nevertheless are aimed at the yachtsman who has at least a smattering of the subject already and wishes to pursue it further.

As a result of these two books, an even more remarkable factor came to light—the interest in the subject of the would-be yachtie and even the average weekend sailor. In response to the flood of requests from these and others who want to start right at the beginning of this fascinating subject, I have written this book as a basic tutor for all who would like to learn the secrets of small boat navigation.

J.E.T.

Chapter 1   **The Chart**

What is a chart?
The whole of coastal navigation is based upon the naval chart.
The chart is, in effect, the mariner's road map. But while there
are many similarities between the familiar road map and the
naval chart, there is also one very big difference between them:

The road map (left) deals solely with the land and virtually
ignores anything to seaward of the coastline.

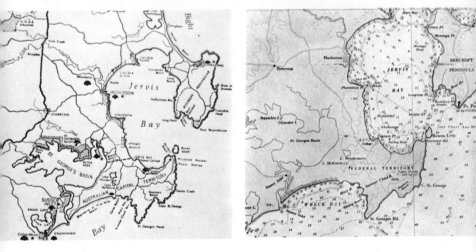

The chart (right) deals solely with the coastline and the sea
and ignores most things inshore of the coastline.

These are very broad descriptions, of course, and there are
exceptions in both cases. The road map, for instance, will carry
details of islands off the coast if there is anything of interest
about them. Similarly, the chart will carry details of mountains, towers or other high objects which may be located well
inland from the coast providing they are visible from sea, and of
use to the marine navigator.

7

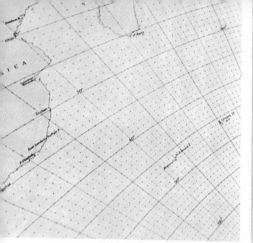

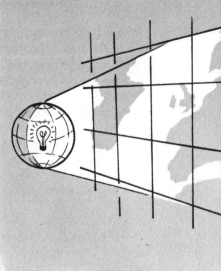

True reproduction of the earth's surface on a flat chart creates distortions of the land areas.

How a chart is made

Again, like a road map, the chart is the representation on a flat sheet of paper of a section of the earth's surface. Because the earth is round, this requires a special construction process to avoid distortion. Imagine part of a tennis ball being flattened. The edges would split and the surface would become distorted.

While it is impossible to flatten all sections of the earth's surface into chart form without such distortions, small areas, particularly if they are not too near the poles, can be successfully reproduced by a method known as Mercator's projection. All modern naval charts used for coastal navigation are made by this projection, and, providing they cover only relatively small areas, there is insufficient distortion to worry about.

Probably the best way to illustrate the projection of the earth's surface onto a flat map is to imagine the globe being transparent, with the land masses marked on it. If a light is placed inside this transparent globe and the whole unit is placed near a wall, the land masses will be projected as shadows onto the flat wall.

Obviously, the distortion will be at its greatest towards the extremities of the wall, so small sections at the very centre of the projection are used to make charts and the distortion is then at a minimum. The globe can be rotated so that each area can be located in the centre and a chart taken off.

8

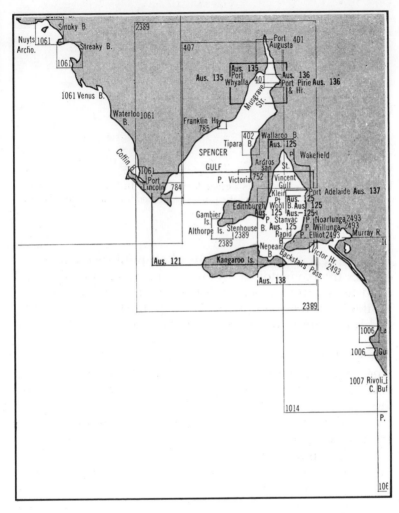

Extract from a typical chart catalogue.

Where charts are obtained

In most countries charts are made by the hydrographic service of the navy. Thus they can almost always be obtained from the navy office. In many ports, particularly where there are no navy establishments, chart agents are appointed. These may be bookshops or suppliers of nautical equipment, and carry limited supplies of naval charts.

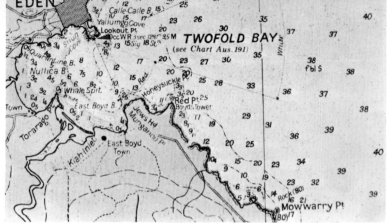

The medium scale chart offers a great deal of detail and is the most widely used chart. Large scale chart of the port is indicated for making an entrance.

A chart catalogue with details of all published charts, enables the navigator to determine at a glance exactly which chart he requires. Special charts for yachtsmen are also available in many countries. Those published by Stanford and Imray are probably best suited to small craft.

The scale of a chart

Since there is a chart for every ocean, every coastline and every port in the world, it follows that there must be charts of differing scales.

On an ocean chart, for example, there would be little need for great detail since, for the most part, the area covers vast open spaces. On an inshore chart, by contrast, fine detail of every inch of the coastline is required so that vessels can navigate safely through the many shoals and hazards.

There are three major scales for naval charts, and each covers a specific area of navigation:

1 Small scale charts cover large stretches of ocean and carry only limited detail of the coastlines.

2 Medium scale charts, which carry sufficient detail along stretches of coastline (say 100 miles or so) to enable a boat to be successfully navigated offshore.

3 Large scale charts, which carry fine detail of virtually every inch of estuaries, ports and rivers, to enable boats unfamiliar with the area to make a safe entry.

Coasting close inshore requires large scale charts with a wealth of detail to make navigation safe.

There are few hazards in the open ocean and charts covering these areas carry relatively little detail of the coastlines.

The would-be navigator, setting off on a passage, can select from the chart catalogue all the charts he will require to cover all aspects of navigation and safety *en route* without cluttering up his boat with unnecessary folios.

If he is making an ocean crossing, for example, he will select the small scale chart to cover the ocean area, two or three medium scale charts to cover his landfall and any coastal passages involved, and large scale charts of his departure and arrival ports or any other places he may visit either for interest or for shelter.

Metric charts

A gradual conversion to metric charts is taking place in many parts of the world. It is currently possible to purchase both

AUSTRALIA – EAST COAST
NEW SOUTH WALES

CLARENCE RIVER
TO
DANGER POINT

900

FROM SURVEYS BY THE ROYAL AUSTRALIAN NAVY TO 1960
Soundings in hairline from British Admiralty charts.
Byron Bay Lt. Ho. Lat. 28°38'24".83 S. Long. 153°38'12"E.
Topography from the Royal Australian Survey Corps.

955

Bearings refer to the True Compass and are given from Seaward (thus:— 126° etc.)
All heights are expressed in feet above Mean High Water Springs
For abbreviations see Admiralty Chart 5011.

1000

SOUNDINGS IN FATHOMS
(Under Eleven in Fathoms and Feet)

Natural Scale $\frac{1}{150,000}$ (at Lat. 28°52·5'S.)   960

Projection   Mercator

Chart title (*above*). Global grid of
Latitude and Longitude (*top
right*). The grid as seen on a chart
(*bottom right*).

fathom and metric charts, sometimes of the same area, often of
the same coastline. Needless to say it is vitally important to the
navigator to know which chart he is using. This information is
carried in the chart title and should be checked when the chart
is purchased.

The chart title

Every chart carries a title with a wealth of information of use to
the navigator. Apart from the obvious description of the area
covered by the chart, other factors relating to the scale, the
soundings, tidal anomalies, military areas, special areas,
specific dangers and any other factors which will assist in safe
navigation are listed in the chart title.

Latitude and longitude

Mercator charts are covered by a 'grid' pattern indicating lines

12

of latitude and longitude which match those on the earth's globe. The lines which run vertically up and down the chart are meridians of longitude, and those which run horizontally across it are parallels of latitude. Their use will be seen in a later chapter when the chart is used for plotting.

The scale across the top and bottom of the chart is the longitude scale and is marked with degrees and minutes of arc (60 minutes = 1 degree). Longitude commences at 0° on the Greenwich meridian (London), and runs east and west 180 degrees to the opposite side of the world. Thus the graduations on the top and bottom of the chart will be in degrees and minutes of longitude east or west of Greenwich and marked accordingly.

On either side of the chart are the graduations for the latitude scale. Latitude commences on the equator and is measured north and south of the poles. The graduations are the same (degrees and minutes) as longitude, but the two are dissimilar in scale and must never be confused. Latitude at the equator is 0° and runs only 90 degrees to the north and south poles.

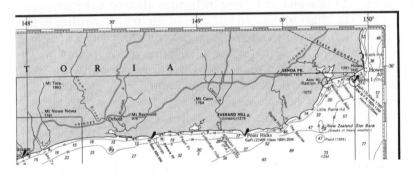

Distance scale

Distances at sea are always measured in nautical miles, and thus the distance scale is the same on every chart regardless of whether it is graduated in metres or fathoms. Any distance scale which may be incorporated in the title—or anywhere on the chart for that matter—can be ignored, since it is related to land miles. The latitude scale on either side of the chart (*never* the longitude scale at top or bottom) is used to measure distance, thus:

One minute of latitude = One nautical mile.

13

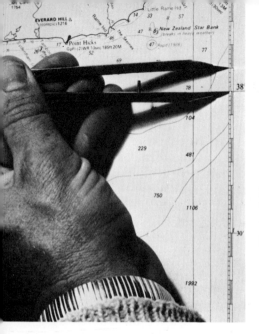

To measure one nautical mile, place the dividers against one unit (one minute) of the latitude scale. It can then be transferred to wherever the measurement is required either horizontally, vertically or diagonally across the chart. Here a distance of 5 nautical miles is measured.

Soundings

The depth of water indicated by figures all across the seaward area of the chart may be in fathoms or metres (according to the chart title). Close inshore these depths may be represented in smaller denominations, either as fathoms and feet or as decimals of a metre. This is probably the most confusing and dangerous aspect in the conversion to metric charts and the navigator must be very aware of it.

The depths are indicated by a normal sized sounding figure with a smaller figure below and to the right of it. They are read off thus:

Fathoms: 5_2 (5 fathoms 2 feet = 32 feet) [1 fathom = 6 feet]
Metres: 5_2 (5.2 metres   = 17 feet approx.)

The danger of confusing the two systems is obvious from this example.

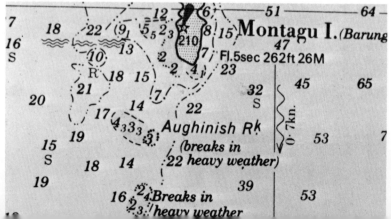

Chart datum represents the structure of the waterway at lowest low tide. Tide heights must be added to chart figures.

The marked depths, known traditionally as soundings, are reduced to the lowest mean low tides experienced in the area. Thus it is safe to say that *with only rare exceptions*, the soundings on the chart indicate the least water over the sea bottom that will be experienced in a normal tidal cycle. Or, to put it more practically, there will rarely be less water than that indicated by the soundings.

Chart datum

This is the term given to the level of soundings on the chart. It is the basis on which all tide tables are calculated. Thus, to find the depth of water over the sea bottom at any time, the height of the tide, from the tide tables, is added to the sounding on the chart. This is described in more detail in a later chapter dealing with tides and tidal streams.

Coloured shading

Modern charts have adopted a system of colour shading to give greater emphasis to certain depths. Particularly is this the case with inshore soundings. Shallow waters are usually indicated by deep blue colouring (green if they dry at low tide), which fades out to paler blue as the water becomes deeper. The land is often shaded yellow or some similar contrasting colour and

15

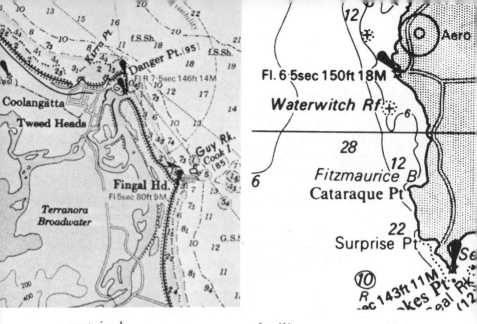

certain danger areas, or areas of military or commercial use, may use pale mauve shading.

Navigation lights, which are the navigator's signposts, as it were, are indicated by a red 'flash'. While there are other shore lights which can be used for navigation, those indicated by the red flash are the only completely reliable navigation beacons.

Contour lines

Although mountains are not used widely for navigation unless they are very prominent or have some particularly obvious characteristic, their presence may be indicated by the usual contour lines used on normal survey maps.

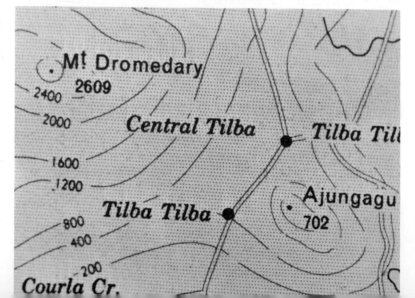

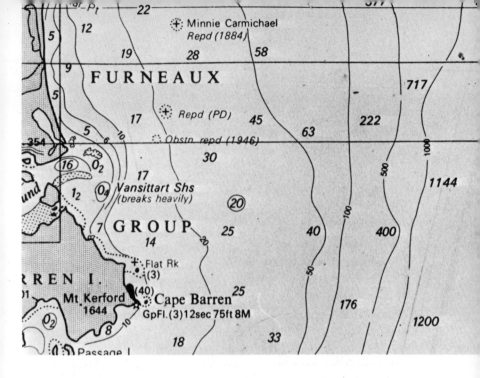

Offshore, the undulations of the sea bed are indicated by contour lines often similar to those of mountains. Another system, however, uses a coded contour line to indicate the variations in depth. The usual code is a series of dots and dashes forming the line of soundings, in which the figure of the depth is indicated by the dots, and the tens (or 'noughts' or 'zeros') by the dashes.

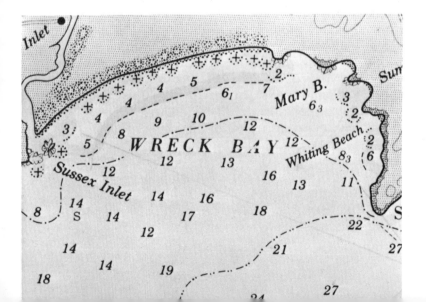

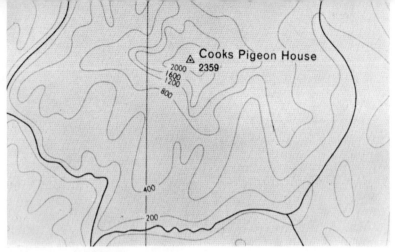

Prominent mountain clearly marked.

Towns, villages etc

Since streets, houses, shops and the general makeup of towns and villages are of no interest to the navigator, they are rarely marked on the chart except in basic form. Particularly is this the case when they are inshore from the coastline. However, any prominent object which can be seen from seaward and used for navigation is pinpointed and marked very distinctly.

Typical of the sort of objects which fall into this category are church steeples, factory chimneys, water towers, radio towers, etc. Indeed, any object anywhere which can be seen clearly from seaward will be marked on the chart.

Details on a chart

One of the biggest problems in constructing a chart is to include all the detail necessary to enable it to be used for safe navigation. The motorist has road signs all along his route to supplement his road map. But there are no signs to assist the boat navigator and all his information must be carried on the chart. To avoid completely cluttering the chart, the wealth of detail relating to both sea and coastline is abbreviated or indicated by symbols.

An illustrated chart or volume, No. 5011 published by the British Hydrographic Office, should be kept aboard every boat. The conscientious navigator, however, will see to it that he knows by heart the more common symbols, particularly those used to indicate dangerous areas.

18

640

Cooks Pigeon House 237° 45 miles

Chart illustration of prominent mountain.

Metric Charts

④ ⌀(4) (4)	⊕(Masts) ⋮(Mast 3m) / ⋮(Funnel) / ⋮(Mast dries 2·1m)	Eddies symbols
1 Rock which does not cover (with elevation above MHWS or MHHW, or where there is no tide, above MSL)	Large scale charts 12 Wreck of which the masts only are visible	19 Eddies
⬡(1₂) ⊙(1₂) ⊙Dries 1·2m ⊙Dr 1·2m ✳(1₂)	(15) Wk	
2 §Rock which covers and uncovers (with elevation above chart datum)	(Oa)Unsurveyed wreck over which the exact depth is unknown but which is considered to have a safe clearance at the depth shown	
✳ ⊛	⊕	20 Kelp
3 Rock awash at the level of chart datum	14 Wreck over which the exact depth of water is unknown but is thought to be 28 metres or less, and which is considered dangerous to surface navigation	21 Bk Bank
		22 Sh Shoal
(1₂) + ⊕ (+ + +) R		23 Rf Reef
		24 Le Ledge
4 Submerged rock with 2 metres or less water over it at chart datum, or rock ledge on which depths are known to be 2 metres or less, or a rock or rock ledge over which the exact depth is unknown but which is considered to be dangerous to surface navigation	(7₃) Wk	
	15 ‡Wreck over which the depth has been obtained by sounding, but not by wire sweep	25 Breakers
(10₇) 16₅ R R	(9₁) Wk	27 Obstn Obstruction
		28 Wk Wreck
5 Shoal sounding on isolated rock	15a‡Wreck which has been swept by wire to the depth shown	29 See 17 Wreckage
		29a See 17 Wreck remains
35 R		30 See 17 Submerged piling
6 Submerged rock not dangerous to surface navigation		30a See 17 Snags; submerged stumps
⊙₄ 11₂	⊹⊢	32 dr Dries
		33 cov Covers
6a Submerged danger with depth cleared by wire drag	16 ‡Wreck over which the exact depth is unknown but thought to be more than 28 metres, or a wreck over which the depth is thought to be 28 metres or less, but which is not considered dangerous to surface vessels capable of navigating in the vicinity.	34 uncov Uncovers
		35 Repd Reported
(˙˙) Historic Wreck ⌐¬ Historic Wreck (see Note) ⌙_ (see Note)		
(Oc) Restricted area round the site of a wreck of historical and archaeological importance.	(˙˙)Foul ⌐Foul⌐ ⌐Foul⌐	38 Limiting danger line
	17 The remains of a wreck, or other foul area, no longer dangerous to surface navigation, but to be avoided by vessels anchoring, trawling, etc.	(Ob) Areas of mobile bottom (including sand waves)
(Covers and uncovers) (Always covered)		41 PA †(PA) Position approximate
10 §Coral reef		42 PD †(PD) Position doubtful
		43 ED †(ED) Existence doubtful
⚓ Wk		See QI Sounding of doubtful depth
Large scale charts		44 posn Position
11 Wreck showing any portion of hull or superstructure at the level of chart datum	18 Overfalls and tide-rips	46 unexamd Unexamined

Typical page of symbols from publication 5011.

Abbreviations

Abbreviations used on a chart are usually in the form of a single capital letter. The letter M, for example, when printed on a stretch of open water, indicates the nature of the sea bottom—mud. If one letter is not sufficient, then two or perhaps three may be used, thus: Tr—tower; Whf—wharf; Bn—beacon.

While abbreviations are often fairly obvious, the same cannot always be said of symbols. A dangerous rock, for example, is illustrated by a small cross, a lighthouse by a tiny stellate. These symbols are all listed in detail in publication 5011, but since there is always the possibility that a copy of this may not be kept on board, or that there is not time to go below and read it up when in narrow or dangerous waters, the wise navigator, as mentioned, will know by heart the more common symbols so that he can identify them quickly on the chart.

The following illustrations are of just such symbols and the objects they represent.

21

Radar prominent areas

The advent of radar, while still limited in small boats, has given the navigator a new string to his bow. Electronic navigation has come into its own in the years since World War II and charts have been kept in line with this development. One of the weaknesses of radar is its tendency to show up different types of objects with different emphasis on the screen. Thus a high cliff will show up clearly while a low scrubby shore-line may not show up at all.

Recent charts have been altered to help overcome this problem by emphasising areas which are 'radar prominent'. These areas of coastline are printed more heavily on the chart and thus stand out against the rest of the coastline, much as they would when viewed on the radar screen.

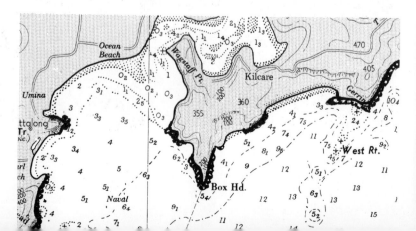

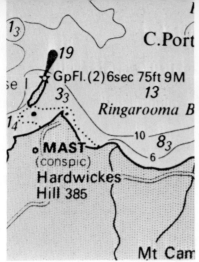

A special feature.　　　　　　　The compass rose.

Special features

Outside the normal symbols and abbreviations there may be
need to convey some special information about an object
marked on the chart. In this case a more expansive abbreviation
than a single letter may be used. Most of these are self-evident.

   An object which stands out well from its surrounding
environment, for example, will be marked with the
abbreviation (*conspic*). An area in which a light cannot be seen
will be zoned and marked (*obscd*) indicating that the light is
obscured in this zone. Similar abbreviations may be used for a
whole variety of objects where there is some special
navigational feature about them.

The compass rose

Since most navigation on a chart involves the use of the compass, a reproduction of a compass card is printed at strategic
points across the face of every chart. These are termed compass
roses and their positioning is such that there is always one close
to hand no matter where on the chart the navigator is working.
They are graduated in three figure notation from 0° to 360°
with a central diagonal grid and contain details of the variation
in force in that area.

   The use of the compass rose for chartwork and the information related to variation are contained in Chapter 3 of this book.

NOTICE TO MARINERS

529 (T). AUSTRALIA—NEW SOUTH WALES—Camden Haven—Works in Progress; Light established.

Former Notice—293 of 1967 (TEMPORARY) cancelled.

(1) The Northern breakwater is being extended in a 073° direction for 650 feet.

(2) The Southern breakwater is being extended in a 073° direction for 150 feet.

(3) A new Southern breakwater is being constructed from a position on the foreshore E. of the Pilot Station flagstaff (31° 38′ 30″ S., 152° 50′ 10″ E. approx.) in a 015½° direction for approximately 1,350 feet or to a position approximately 450 feet S.E. of the completed seaward extension of the Northern breakwater.

(4) A light *Fl. R. 1M.* will be exhibited at the seaward end of the new breakwater construction when within 300 feet of the line of leads.

(5) During these works the channel carrying the best water is variable and caution be exercised in crossing the bar without local knowledge.

(*15th November, 1968*)

Chart temporarily affected—Aus. 811.

Maritime Services Board of New South Wales. (*A.H. 61/50.*)

Hydrographic Office,
Department of the Navy,
Garden Island,
Sydney, N. S. W.

A. H. COOPER,
Hydrographer, R. A. N

V. C. N. Blight, Government Printer, New South Wales—1968

Typical *Notice to Mariners.*

Correcting the chart

Like all maps, charts can quickly become outdated by changes to the coastline or to navigational objects. Removal of a prominent shore object such as a radio tower or chimney, for example, or changes in the light shown from a lighthouse due to maintenance are but two factors which could cause confusion to the offshore navigator.

Such changes are published weekly in a sort of news sheet produced by the navy and called the *Notice to Mariners*. From the details in these notices, the navigator can correct his chart and keep it up to date with events which may affect his navigation. Permanent changes are made on the chart in purple ink, temporary changes in pencil.

Details of every facet of a river or estuary are among the many items contained in the *Sailing Directions*.

Whenever a change is made on the chart, the number of the *Notice to Mariners* is entered in the margin, at the bottom of the chart. In this way, a glance at the listed numbers will indicate the extent to which the chart has been corrected. Chart agents will correct a chart for a fee, and it is a wise precaution before setting off on an extended passage to submit all charts to the chart agents for updating.

Sailing directions

Also known as 'pilots', these are publications put out either by the Admiralty or local authorities. While they are not a part of the chart, they are directly associated with it in that they supplement the information given on the chart. As the navigator progresses along a coastline, the chart gives him a 'moving picture', as it were, of the area. The *Sailing Directions* can then be thought of as the soundtrack to that 'movie'.

This publication goes into all the finer points of the coastal scene in detail which cannot be carried on the chart due to space limitations. It is therefore vital that an up-to-date issue of the *Sailing Directions* is carried aboard on any coastal passage. Corrections and changes to the *Sailing Directions* are also found in the *Notices to Mariners*.

Chapter 2   Navigation Equipment

Before even leaving the mooring to make a coastal passage, the navigator has many things to do. Firstly he must plan the passage to ensure that the boat makes the shortest trip consistent with safety. Then he must ensure that she is ready for the trip in terms of navigational equipment and charts. He must satisfy himself in regard to currents and tides, weather and other factors which may affect the boat during the course of her passage.

Perhaps the first thing which can be done well in advance is to ensure that she is fitted with the correct navigational gear to enable him not only to lay off her courses, but also to plot her track and keep a check of her progress as the passage proceeds.

There is a lot of preparation work behind making a coastal passage.

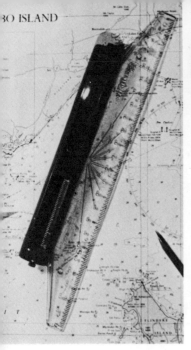

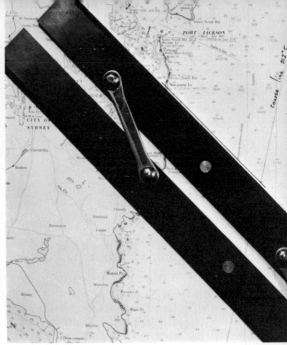

Roller rules.   'Clackety-clacks'!

Chart instruments

Parallel rules

These are double-edged rules which are used to transfer courses
and bearings across the chart. They are essential for coastal
navigation and can be obtained in two principal forms—
sliding rules (sometimes known as 'clackety-clacks') which
shuffle across the surface of the chart, or roller rules which are,
as their name denotes, fitted with small rollers to enable them
to be rolled parallel across the chart.

For small boats the roller type is probably more suitable since
the sliding type tends to stick on any wet spot on the chart, and
there would be few small boats which do not get water on the
chart at some stage in a coastal passage.

By placing one edge of the parallel rules against a line or
against a compass bearing, the line can be transferred to any
part of the chart simply by moving the rules gently across the
surface. Patent types of rules for laying off courses are also
available and these can be quite useful if one becomes adjusted
to using them.

Dividers

These are used for measuring distances, as described in Chapter 1 and are as essential as the parallel rules. The 'one-handed' variety illustrated are the easiest to use and make a good span to cover long jumps along the course line.

A pair of compasses

Not to be confused with the marine or magnetic compasses, these are simply the compasses from the school geometry box used for drawing circles. Handy during the laying off of courses.

Pencils and rubber

These are pretty obvious assets, but it is important to note that the pencil should be 2B grade or softer. Charts are made of fairly tough cartridge paper to facilitate easy rubbing off when plotting is finished, but if a hard pencil is used, an imprint may be left on the surface of the chart which will be hard to eradicate.

Stop watch

Handy for timing the cycle of lights.

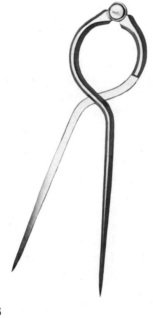

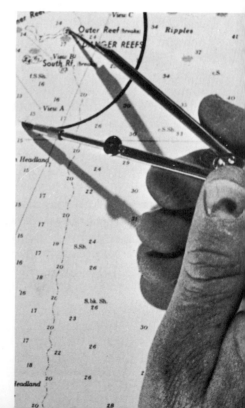

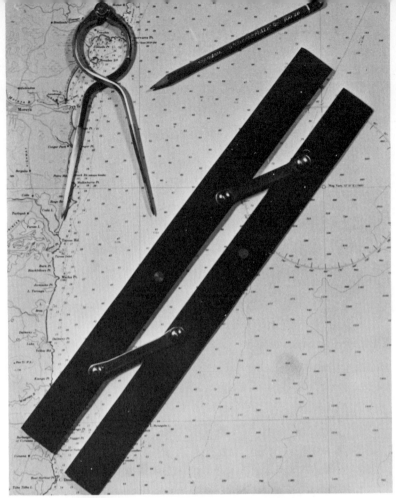

The simple requirements for chartwork.

Chart table

The size and fitting of a chart table will depend on the size and roominess of the boat. Some navigators work on the saloon table, others have specially fitted navigation areas with properly established chart tables. But for the average small yacht, a flat surface roughly the dimensions of half a chart is all that is required and this can be fixed temporarily over a bunk or some similar spot.

The half-chart size enables the chart to be folded just once thus avoiding too many creases on its surface while permitting

29

Simple chart table for a small yacht.

reasonable working room. An underlay of flat rubber sheeting between the chart and the table prevents the paper slipping or the table getting marked by pricks from the dividers. A 'fiddle' or raised edge prevents everything sliding to the deck whenever the boat heels.

Electronic instruments

Depth sounder

At one time, the depth of the water was found by use of a 'lead line'—a marked line with a weight at one end. The weighted end was dropped into the water until it touched bottom and the depth measured off the line where it broke the surface. A few lead lines are still in use, but for the most part boats nowadays use the electronic depth sounder for finding the depth of the water under the keel.

This sounder works on the principle of an electronic pulse which is transmitted from a spot on the bottom of the boat. When this pulse reaches the sea bed, it 'echoes' back and is picked up by a receiver, also in the bottom of the boat. The instrument then measures the time taken for the pulse to echo and reads off the depth of the water on a scale.

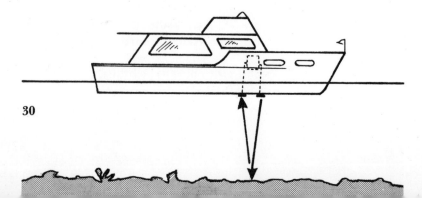

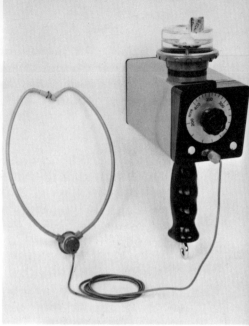

Above: Depth sounder with dial and recorder.

Right: A small boat RDF unit.

There are two main forms of depth scales: a dial which has a neon 'blip' to indicate the depths, and a continuous roll of graph paper, rather like a barograph, on which a stylus draws a trace of the bottom of the sea as the boat passes over it. Both systems are useful, and both accurate, although the trace method is preferred by most professional navigators.

Radio direction finder

Known as RDF, this is an electronic means of taking a direction bearing off a shore transmitter. The transmitter sends out a continuous coded signal, the type and frequency of which can be found in the *List of Radio Signals*. On board the boat, this signal is picked up by a special receiver with a tuneable aerial. As the aerial is turned, the signal fades away until it dies out altogether then, as the aerial continues to turn, fades up again.

The direction of the station is found when the signal cuts out at the bottom of the 'dip', and by means of a nearby compass, a bearing can be taken and plotted on the chart (see Chapter 6). Much the same effect can be obtained with a simple transistor radio tuned in to a commercial station. The 'loop' aerial inside the transistor causes the audio signal to increase and fade as the set is turned towards and away from the station.

Commercial radio stations may be used at a push, but this is not advisable. Special RDF transmitters are set up along the coastline and often linked together so that the navigator can obtain a series of bearings of different stations and thus plot his position.

The log

As with the depth sounder, the electronic log is a relatively recent addition to small boat equipment. Previously the distance a boat travelled through the water was recorded by a spinner on the end of a line dragged behind the boat. As the spinner turned, it twisted the line which, in turn, recorded the 'twisted' distance on a dial at the stern of the boat. These logs, known as the 'Walker Log', are still used today and are surprisingly accurate.

Most electronic logs depend on a small impeller being attached to the hull of the boat. As the hull moves through the water the impeller turns and the distance is recorded on a dial somewhere in the boat. These logs may sometimes be driven mechanically by means of a twisting cable, but most are connected electronically. The dial records the distance travelled and sometimes also the speed of the boat, rather along the lines of a car odometer.

Radar

One of the most useful of all electronic navigation instruments, radar is only just beginning to make an impact on the small boat field. Previously it was too big, too bulky and far too

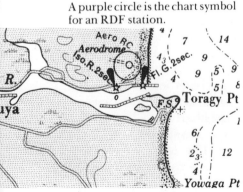

A purple circle is the chart symbol for an RDF station.

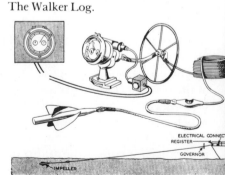

The Walker Log.

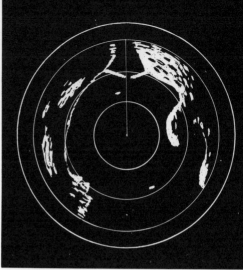

expensive for all but luxury yachts, but transistor technology has reduced its bulk, and mass production has brought down the price to acceptable levels so that nowadays the average yacht or motor cruiser can fit a small radar set.

Radar works on much the same principle as the depth sounder in that it transmits an electronic pulse and times the echo. The difference lies, however, in that the radar set works above water—usually fairly high up on the boat—and transmits its pulse in a 360° circle. The echo from surrounding objects is not recorded as a figure on a dial or as a trace, but is laid out in the form of a map of the surrounding area with the boat in the centre.

Obviously, this makes life very easy for the navigator, for a glance at the radar screen can tell him just where the boat is positioned in relation to the surrounding coastline, and he can compare this with an identical chart. If he wishes, he can also take off bearings and distances of prominent objects in order to plot the boat's position accurately.

As mentioned in Chapter 1 however, radar is prone to one weakness in that it tends to echo badly off certain terrain. Thus the picture on the screen is not always an accurate one and needs to be interpreted so that mistakes are not made. Modern charts are marked to indicate which areas offer best radar 'echoes'.

Chapter 3   The Marine Compass

The gyro compass

This is without doubt the best type of compass for marine work and is fitted to most commercial and naval vessels. Unfortunately it is not easily adapted to small boat use, mainly because of its complex makeup. The compass comprises a free spinning gyroscope wheel which aligns itself in the true north/south line. Its advantages lie in its freedom from the errors which plague the magnetic compass, but its drawbacks lie in the difficulty of fitting and maintaining such complex equipment in the framework of a small boat. For this reason, the magnetic compass will be dealt with solely in this book.

The magnetic compass

In its most basic form, the magnetic compass can be considered to be the needle-type 'Boy Scout' compass familiar in so many different sports. The needle, which is itself magnetised, lies in the magnetic field of the earth in such a way that it points towards the magnetic north pole no matter how the compass bowl is turned.

The marine compass

The principal difference between a needle compass and the marine compass is that in the latter the swinging needle is replaced by a swinging card. This is purely to allow easier reading of the compass when the boat is moving around in a seaway, for basically both compasses are the same. Instead of using a needle moving across a card, the marine compass has a free swinging card to which magnetic needles are attached with their north pointing end in line with the north point on the compass card. When the needles swing to take up their magnetic north/south line, they swing the card with them.

A big ship gyro compass.

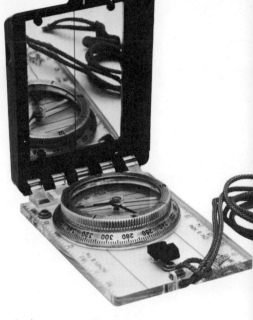

An inexpensive but accurate
'needle' type compass.

An ideal small yacht compass.

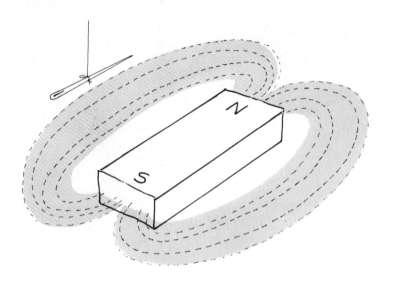

Earth's magnetic field

To understand how a marine compass is used it is necessary to understand the basic magnetic field of an ordinary magnet. The analogy of the sheet of iron filings used in the school physics lab is a good one. When a magnet is placed beneath the sheet of iron filings, they form themselves into a pattern illustrating the lines of magnetic force radiating from one pole to the other. The needle of a compass placed within this field will align itself with the lines of force that surround it.

Now think of the world as the magnet. The lines of force radiate similarly from the poles and the needle of a compass placed within earth's field will align itself with these lines of magnetic force. Since they emanate from north and south poles, the needle will align itself in the north/south direction. Unfortunately the magnetic poles are not situated in the same place as the true poles and thus an error occurs in the true reading of the compass.

Variation

This is the name given to the error caused by the difference in position between the true and magnetic poles. As its name denotes, it varies from place to place across the world, but it is accurately tabulated for the navigator's use. It can be described as follows:

Variation is the error in the compass caused by the earth's magnetism. It is always named E or W according to which direction the card is deflected away from the true north.

Deviation

The second of the two errors which affect the magnetic compass, deviation, is caused by the magnetic influence of anything near the compass needle. Someone placing a metal knife alongside the binnacle, for example, will cause a deflection of the compass needle and result in a deviation error. Steel in the construction of the boat, electric circuits, motors, and so on, can all affect the compass and create a deviation error. It would be safe to describe this error as follows:

Deviation is the error in the compass caused by the boat's magnetism. It is always named E or W according to the direction the card is deflected from true north.

To find variation error

This is easy. On every chart there are a number of compass roses as described in Chapter 1. In the centre of each compass rose is listed the variation for that area and the amount it is likely to change in one year, which is usually fairly small.

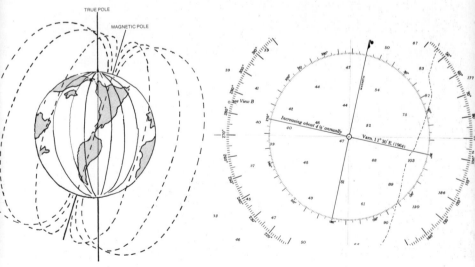

Earth's magnetic field.

Variation is written across the compass rose.

To find deviation error

This is not so easy. To begin with, every new fitting, new stores or new equipment placed on the boat can add to the error of deviation. Providing the new products are not too magnetic and they are kept at least 1 metre away from the compass binnacle, they should not have too much effect, and this is worth remembering when fitting out a boat.

The deviation can change with each change in the boat's direction, which creates another problem. Finally, the boat itself, particularly if she is of steel construction, will have become a magnet in her own right during her building period and, as can well be imagined, this will play havoc with the accuracy of the compass in the binnacle.

The best way to find the deviation error is to engage a professional compass adjuster and have him attempt to eliminate the error, or if it cannot be eliminated, then tabulate it on what is known as a deviation card.

Large motor cruisers and yachts with steel hulls are most susceptible to deviation problems.

DEVIATION CARD

VESSEL *Cygnet* TYPE *24' Sloop*

BOAT'S HEAD		DEVIATION
N	000°	0°
NE	045°	1° East
E	090°	2° East
SE	135°	1° East
S	180°	0°
SW	225°	1° West
W	270°	2° West
NW	315°	1° West
N	360°	0°

The deviation card

When a boat is checked for deviation she must be checked on all headings since, as mentioned, deviation varies according to the course being steered. The compass adjuster will swing the boat through the major compass points and determine the deviation on each point. He will then list the deviation error on each heading on a deviation card, a sample of which is given below. Thus the navigator can, by referring to this card, determine his deviation error on whatever course he is planning to steer.

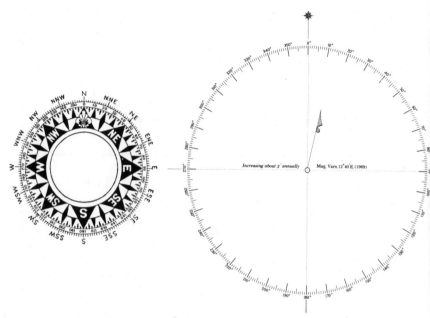

The compass card

For many years the traditional mariner's compass carried a card
on which were ornately printed the cardinal points of the compass as well as three figure notation. Modern compasses,
however, have mostly done away with this cardinal system and
have only three figure notation (0°-360°) inscribed on the edge
of the card.

The card commences at 0° (due north) and travels in one
degree units through 090° (due east), 180° (south), 270° (west)
back to 360° or 0° at due north.

The lubber line

The lubber line is the term given to the mark on the bowl of the
compass which represents the centreline of the boat. Thus,
when steering a course, the card is swung until the figure
representing the course lies against the lubber line.

The master compass

This is the compass situated in the cockpit by which all courses
are steered. It is usually the largest and most accurate compass
in the boat and is mounted in a binnacle with screening and
lighting to make reading easier at night.

The lubber line indicates a compass
reading of 234°.

The master compass is always located
near the helm.

The repeater or tell-tale compass

Any small compass situated elsewhere in the boat—on the flybridge of a cruiser, above the skipper's bunk or on the navigator's table—is referred to as a tell-tale compass. They are sometimes referred to as repeater compasses.

The hand-bearing compass

The most useful compass on small boats other than the master compass, the hand-bearing compass, is completely portable and can be used in a variety of places around the boat. As its name denotes, it is used for obtaining bearings and since, particularly on a heeling yacht, it is not always possible to obtain bearings from the cockpit, it may be carried to any strategic position where clear bearings can be taken.

Usually this compass is fairly small and light and has a handle for convenience when holding. Since it is used mostly at eye level, it is often fitted with a prism or mirror as well as with a sight, not unlike a rifle sight.

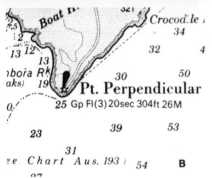

Boat Hr.

Crocod.le

34

32

4

13 12
13

bora Rk
aks) 19

30

50

Pt. Perpendicular

0.

25 Gp Fl(3) 20sec 304ft 26M

23

39

53

31

e Chart Aus. 193) 54

B

A. A shore object (lighthouse) is selected.
B. Identified on the chart.
C. Sighted over the hand bearing compass (but not yet in alignment).
D. Lubber line, sight and object lined up. Bearing reads 187°C.

Taking a compass bearing

A shore object, of which a bearing is to be taken, is first
identified on the chart. The hand-bearing compass is then held
up to eye level until this object appears in the 'v' sight. The
lubber line and the figures on the relevant section of the compass card are reflected in the prism or mirror directly below this
sight. When the object, 'v' sight, lubber line and compass
figures are all in alignment, the figure against the lubber line is
read off as the compass bearing off the object.

43

Liquid damped compasses

Because of the violent motion of a small boat in a seaway, the compass card is liable to charge around on its pivot making it almost impossible for the helmsman to follow. For this reason most marine compasses are filled with liquid and fitted with a 'damped' device which slows the swing of the card and absorbs the violence of the boat's movement, thus making steering and navigation easier and more accurate. Dry card compasses are not really suitable for small craft.

Compass error

As described earlier in this chapter, every boat is affected by variation and deviation. A good compass adjuster will eliminate the deviation if it is small, but, unfortunately, this is not always possible and both errors are present. They are known collectively as compass error.

The drawings below illustrate what can happen to a boat which does not allow for compass error and how such error can be applied so that the boat may steer her required course.

Let's assume that we are fishing on an offshore reef when the weather turns thick and we are unable to see the shoreline. We know that the course (taken from the chart) back to port is 270° and we have a compass error of, say 15°W. If we do not allow for the error, but steer the course of 270° on the compass, the error will push the boat 15° off course and she will wind up wrecked on the coastline to the south of the port entrance.

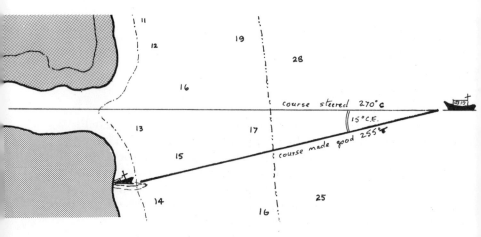

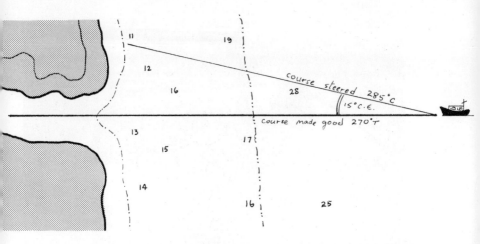

By allowing the compass error the boat, although steering 15° to the north of the port entrance, will be pushed back 15° by the error and make a true course of 270° right into the harbour.

Compass error is computed by adding or subtracting the variation to the deviation as follows:

LIKE NAMES ADD: UNLIKE NAMES SUBTRACT

Thus: Variation 10°E Deviation 2°W = Compass Error 8°E.
Variation 10°E Deviation 2°E = Compass Error 12°E.

Applying the compass error

Since everything on the chart is drawn to the *true* north, and everything done by compass is related to magnetic or *compass* north it follows that between working on the chart and applying those workings in practice to the compass, the error must be allowed.

Think of it this way: the chart table is down below on most yachts. The compass (either steering or hand-bearing) is up on deck. Thus every time the navigator goes up or down the companion way between the deck and the cabin, he must apply the compass error. Making this a habit can eliminate the very easy possibility of forgetting the error and placing the boat in danger.

Applying the compass error can be done in a number of ways, notably by diagrams. But the easiest way to avoid confusion,

Unless compass error is allowed correctly, the boat will be steering many degrees off course.

and one which is absolutely foolproof, is to remember the jingle:

ERROR EAST, COMPASS LEAST—ERROR WEST, COMPASS BEST

An example is probably the best way to illustrate the use of this jingle:

Variation	10°E	True course on the chart	269°T
Deviation	3°W	Error	7°E
			(error east
			compass least)
Error	7°E	Course to steer by compass	262°C
Variation	10°E	True course from chart	269°T
Deviation	17°W	Error	7°W
			(error west
			compass best)
Error	7°W	Course to steer by compass	276°C

Be very careful when applying the error to compass bearings taken on the hand-bearing compass (i.e. coming down the companion way!) before laying them off on the chart as the system appears to be reversed:

Variation	10°E	Bearing taken on compass	167°C
Deviation	5°E	Error	15°E
			(error east compass least)
Error	15°E	Bearing to lay off on chart	182°T

It is a wise precaution always to indicate chart bearings and courses with a T (true) and compass bearings and courses with C (compass). This prevents any confusion which might otherwise arise.

Swinging for compass

It sometimes happens that the services of a compass adjuster are not available to find the deviation. When this is the case the navigator must do it himself by a procedure known as swinging for compass. The following are the steps that should be followed:

1 Locate two transit objects (objects in line) and determine their true bearing on the chart.

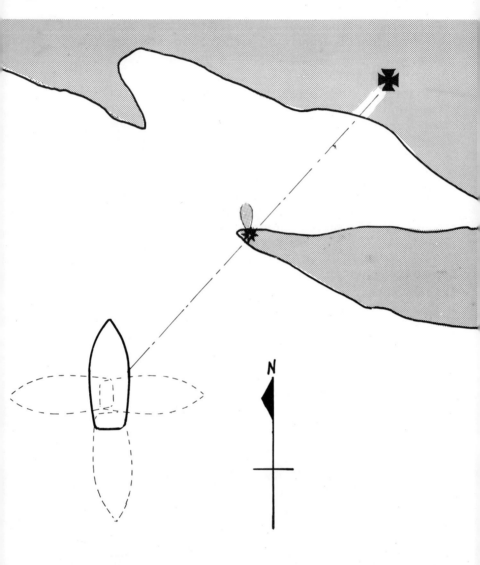

2 Secure the boat at anchor or to a buoy so that these transits are
exactly aligned. By means of a motor or row boat, swing the
boat's head until it is pointing due north.
3 Read off the transit bearing on the compass and apply the
variation.
4 The difference between this result and the true transit bearing is the deviation on this heading. If the true bearing is

greater, the deviation is named east, if it is the lesser, the deviation is named west.

5 Repeat the procedure taking transit bearings on each of the cardinal points.

6 From the results, make up a deviation card as illustrated on page 39.

Note: Because the electrical circuits of the motor may create a deviation error, it is a wise precaution to carry out this procedure first with the motor running and then with it stopped.

Chapter 4 Lights and Lighthouses

Lights are the navigator's signposts. Without them, the job of keeping track of the boat's progress along the course line would be much more difficult. By day the lighthouse buildings offer readily identifiable objects from seaward and for this reason are usually painted white. By night, the light they contain offers almost the sole visible means of navigation on otherwise dark stretches of coastline.

Types of lights
There are three principal types of lights used for coastal navigation:
1 *The ocean light,* which is usually situated near a major port or at some strategic point along the coastline.
2 *The coastal light,* which leads the navigator into the immediate vicinity of a port or estuary.
3 *The harbour light,* which, in an infinite number of varieties, guides the navigator through the shoals and hazards of inshore waterways.

The ocean light

This is a long range light, usually white in colour and showing over a wide arc of the horizon. Its purpose is mainly to assist navigators making offshore passages up and down a coastline or to guide them towards the proximity of a harbour entrance. Its range varies, but 20-25 miles is fairly standard, and each light is usually strategically placed so that as one is left behind, the navigator making a passage along the coastline is not left too long in the dark, as it were, before another appears over the horizon.

To assist identification, these lights have very different characteristics. Although some may be coloured, as a general rule colour inhibits their range and for the most part they show a white light. This light is divided into flashes or groups of flashes shown over differing periods of time so that one light will not be confused with another (see 'characteristic of a light', later this chapter).

For ease of identification by day the lighthouses are usually placed right on the edge of the coastline or on an offshore island, and are distinctive in shape and colour. Stripes and squares are sometimes used to differentiate one from another where they are close together. But where they cannot be confused, the classical tall white 'needle' building is most common.

Coastal lights

Usually placed on headlands at the entrance to a port or some other strategic position, these are the lights that take up where the big ocean lights leave off. They invariably mark the approaches to a harbour, river or channel so that the navigator, having manoeuvred inshore by means of the ocean light, can pick up the coastal light and make his way into the estuary or harbour entrance.

These lights are usually of limited range—say ten miles or less—and often use colours, either as a warning of inshore dangers or as a guide into the channels. Red, green and white are the most commonly used colours with red a particular favourite to indicate dangers. They take many forms, most common of which is the 'sectored' light described later in this chapter.

The structure bearing the light may be anything from the classical lighthouse building to a small iron framework supporting the light itself.

Harbour lights

As their name denotes, these are the lights which mark the channels, shoals and reefs of navigable harbours and estuaries. Their most common form is as channel marking buoys although they can take any colour or shape, and much will depend on the importance of the channel they mark and its use for commercial shipping.

Harbour lights are principally green, white and red but other colours, such as blue, are not unknown. They have a very limited range, often only a mile or so and are invariably unattended. Because they are often set against a background of shore lights, their characteristics may vary greatly from a basic fixed, steady light, to one flashing morse code combinations.

Navigation by day is relatively easy, but if entering a port at night the navigator must be certain of his lights.

Making port with the lights

The offshore navigator, making into a port at night, will follow a routine somewhat similar to that followed by an aircraft pilot on approaching an airport. Just as the aircraft homes in on a beacon near the city, so the boat navigator homes in on the ocean light near the entrance to the port. An aircraft closing in on the airport is offered a guidance pattern from the control tower, whereas the boat navigator uses the guiding pattern of the coastal lights to make his way into the entrance. As the aircraft touches down between two rows of runway lights so the boat is steered to her berth through two rows of channel marking lights.

The loom of a light

Long range ocean lights usually depend on the concentration of *Fresnel* lenses to condense their light into a strong beam. These lenses rotate mechanically, thus sweeping the beam around the horizon like a probing searchlight. As the beam passes a boat offshore, it is seen from the boat as a brilliant flash, again like being swept by a searchlight.

On clear nights, long before the light appears over the horizon, the sweeping beams can be seen in the sky ahead. This is known as the 'loom' of the light, and apart from allowing early identification of the light itself, can be used for plotting the boat's position (see Chapter 6).

The break of the light

At the moment that the loom gives way to the light itself—just like a car headlight coming over a hill—the light appears as a brilliant flash. This is known as the 'break' of the light.

Range of a light

Alongside the light symbol on a chart is the abbreviated characteristic which indicates its performance. Included in this characteristic is the range of the light in nautical miles.

Obviously, the light will be seen at differing distances from different heights above the deck of the boat. So for the range entered on the chart, a standard 'height of eye' of about 5 metres is used. For navigators with a height of eye above sea level other than 5 metres, the range of the light will vary accordingly.

A table called the *Extreme Range Table* enables the range of any light at any height of eye to be calculated.

Height of a light

The height of a light is also included in the details carried on the chart. It has a number of uses in navigation. To allow for a safety margin, heights on a chart are all measured above *mean high water springs*, which is roughly the highest high water of the tidal cycle.

Loom   Break

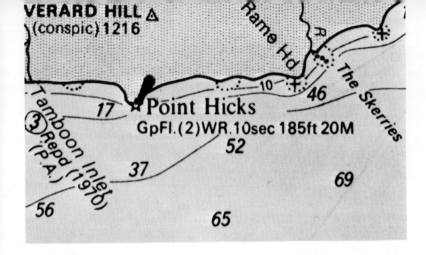

Characteristic of a light

The characteristic of a light is the makeup of its cycle in terms of flashes; their number, duration and timing. With so many lights in sight on a busy coastline (to say nothing, of course, of shore lights) confusion would reign if any of the lights had similar flashing characteristics. Thus in order to prevent such confusion no two lights with similar characteristics are located close together.

There are three principal forms of characteristic used for navigation lights. They are given below together with the abbreviation used to describe them on the chart:

F	Fixed	Constant light with no break.
Fl	Flashing	The period of light is shorter than the period of darkness.
Occ	Occulting	The period of light is longer than the period of darkness.

These three basic characteristics can be again broken down by forming the flashes or the occults into groups. The light is then said to be Group Flashing or Group Occulting and the number in each group may vary up to four. Thus:

Gp Fl (3)   A group of three short flashes followed by a long period of darkness.

Gp Occ (2)   A group of two long occults followed by only a brief period of darkness.

To prevent confusion even further, colours may be added to the characteristic of the light in which case the colour will be indicated by the inclusion of its capital letter. Where the light is solely white, no capital letter is used.

Gp Fl (4) WRG   A light flashing in groups of four in red, or green.

To make absolutely sure there is no confusion, especially when only white is used, the characteristic of the light is further given a time cycle totally different to any other light in the area. This is noted in seconds in the characteristic abbreviation on the chart and includes the *whole* cycle of the light.

Where group flashing or occulting is concerned, the timing of the cycle commences at the beginning of the first flash of one group and ends at the beginning of the first flash in the next group. Thus:

Gp Fl (3) ev. 10 secs.   A group flashing light with three short flashes followed by a long period of darkness, the whole cycle taking ten seconds.

Sectored lights

The most popular form of coastal light leading boats into an

In order to prevent confusion by day, lighthouses are painted with distinctive colours and patterns.

estuary or harbour, or marking offshore or inshore hazards is the sectored light. This uses two or more colours, divided into sectors to indicate to the navigator just where he is in relation to the entrance or to the danger.

As a general rule, the white sector is the safe one, but this should be checked on the chart where the sectors are indicated by pecked lines. The navigator entering a harbour in the white light and seeing it suddenly turn red or green may be sure he has wandered from the safe channel and should immediately check his position.

The sectors are accurate and thus reference to the chart when a sectored light changes colour will indicate the location of the boat somewhere along the sector line. Since the different sectors are obtained by screening the light, the flashing or occulting characteristic of the light is the same regardless of colour.

57

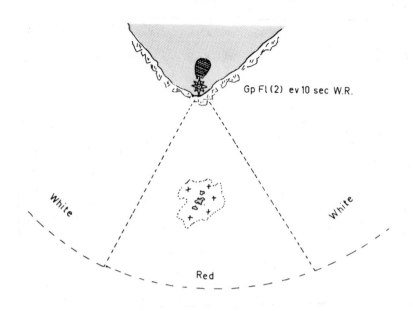

Gp Fl (2) ev 10 sec W.R.

White

White

Red

Some ocean lights use coloured sectors to indicate offshore danger, and once again reference to the chart will indicate the nature of the problem and the colour of the light which covers it. It is not uncommon for the main ocean light to be separate from the coloured sector which might otherwise inhibit its range. In this case both characteristics are included on the chart.

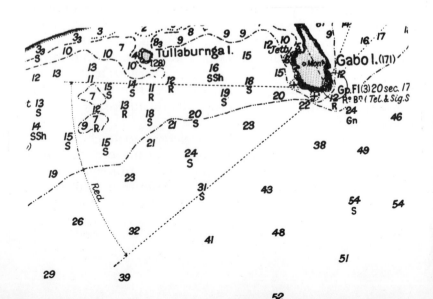

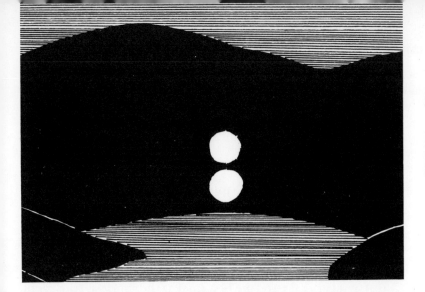

Lead lights

A more accurate method of leading a boat in through a narrow or difficult entrance is the system known as lead lights. These are used widely in canals or rivers where the broader beam of the sectored lights is not sufficiently accurate for the fine navigation required.

Lead lights comprise two individual lights, usually coloured, and placed so that the lower light is in front of the upper. These two lights are lined up so that on entering the channel the navigator sees both lights, one above the other. Any tendency for the boat to stray to starboard will cause the lower light to move to the left of the upper and vice versa. To maintain the centre of the channel the navigator must manoeuvre the boat to keep both lights exactly in line.

By day, brightly coloured marks replace the lights and the same procedure is followed. This is a particularly good system where channels are subject to change due to shifting sand bars or river floods. By moving the lower light, the two lights can be realigned to the new direction of the channel. It is a system widely used to mark the entrance to a river over a dangerous bar.

Chapter 5 **Planning the Coastal Passage**

A passage along a coastline must be carefully planned beforehand so that the boat makes the best possible track consistent with safety. The best track may not always be the shortest, since it may be advantageous to divert in order to gain the assistance of a favourable current or to avoid a dangerous area in unfavourable weather conditions.

But as a general rule, the best track is the shortest, consistent, as mentioned, with safety. So, assuming that there are no hazards *en route*, the planned course from the port of departure to the port of arrival will be a straight line. If there are dangers or hazards on the way, then the best track will probably be a composite course made up of shorter courses designed to pass a safe distance off the dangers.

Departure! And the excitement of a coastal passage to look forward to.

Arrival off the destination port after a successful passage.

Arrival and departure points

Obviously, trying to lay off a series of courses for the boat to
follow through the intricate channels of a harbour or estuary is
virtually impossible. Avoiding collision with other vessels is
just one way that such planned tracks would be upset.

So generally speaking, any navigation within the confines of
a harbour is visual, using the channel markers and buoys to
make the best path down harbour and out into the open sea.

Once clear of the restrictions of sheltered water, however, the
track can be planned along the coastline with little fear of
interference. For this reason, all coastal navigation commences
at a point *outside* the port of departure and terminates at a
predetermined point *outside* the arrival port. Such points are
called, respectively, *departure* and *arrival* points.

It is from the departure point that navigation along the coast
begins. The distance log is set at zero and all calculations are
commenced at this point. A fix is made of the boat's position
when on the departure point (see Chapter 6), and the passage
recorded as starting at that time.

The arrival point is an arbitrary spot somewhere close to the
entrance of the arrival port and clear of any inshore dangers.
The course line, or course lines, for the coastal passage com-
mence at the departure point and terminate at the arrival point.

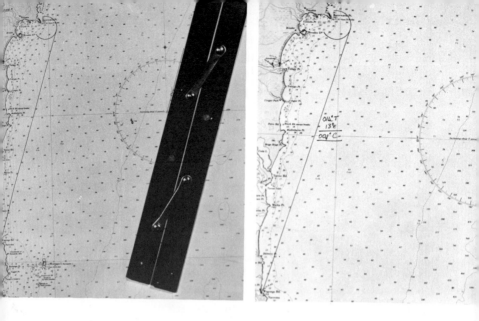

Laying off a course

With the departure and arrival positions established and plotted on the chart, and presuming that one course can be steered for the full length of the passage, finding the course to steer is a simple process:

1. Join the departure and arrival positions with a straight line.
2. Place the parallel rules along this line. Carefully transfer it through the centre of the nearest compass rose.
3. At the point where the edge of the rules cuts the circumference of the compass rose *in the direction in which the boat is to travel*, read off the true course to steer.
4. Convert to a compass course by applying the compass error. This is the course to steer by compass between departure and arrival points, and to make good the track laid off on the chart.

Danger circles

If the course laid between departure and arrival points is clear of all hazards, then no problems arise. But if there are dangers *en route*, or if the course has to round a headland or island, then the navigator must determine beforehand how far off such dangers he wishes to pass.

Much will depend, of course, on conditions. Rounding a

rocky island, for example, in daylight and clear weather conditions, he may pass within half a mile. The same hazard in foul weather or at night may require a clearance of 2 or 3 miles.

Here only the navigator's skill and experience can determine what is a safe distance under the prevailing conditions. Having decided on this safe distance, a 'danger circle' is drawn around the object as follows:

1 Set the compasses with radius the safe distance off the hazard, using the latitude scale.
2 With the point of the compasses on the outermost part of the danger, draw an arc of a circle to seaward of it.
3 Providing the boat stays outside this circle she will always be more than the safe distance off the hazard.
4 From the departure point, draw the first course line at a tangent to this danger circle. This is the course to steer to clear the danger by the predetermined safe distance.

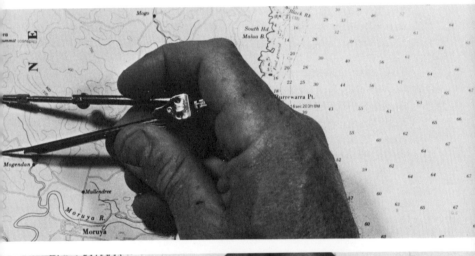

Laying off a composite course

Where the course between departure and arrival points cannot be drawn as one straight line due to intervening hazards, the following procedure is adopted:

1 Draw a danger circle around the first hazard *en route*.
2 Repeat with each hazard (or headland) the boat has to clear before reaching her destination.
3 From the departure point draw the first course at a tangent to the first danger circle as described above.
4 Join the first and second danger circles with a line at a tangent to each.
5 Repeat the procedure until the last danger circle is reached.
6 Draw the final course to the arrival point from a tangent to the last danger circle.
7 Read off the various courses on the compass rose, as described earlier in this chapter, convert to compass by applying compass error, and mark on the chart against each course line.
8 These are the courses to steer in order to make the shortest passage between departure and arrival points while passing all hazards at the predetermined safe distance.

Fog, rain and snow (bad visibility)

It goes without saying that in planning his boat's passage, particularly with regard to passing a safe distance off hazards and dangers, the navigator assumes the weather will be fine and clear. However, in the course of sailing that passage, the weather may well deteriorate and in this case the allowances for a safe distance off the hazards will need to be increased.

Since no navigator, however experienced, can predict exactly what the weather is going to do in the course of the passage, it is more than likely the entire route will need to be redrawn if bad

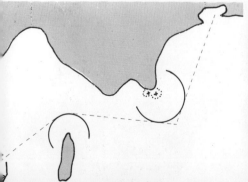

A composite course.

Navigating is relatively easy when weather conditions are good.

A lee shore is always dangerous, even in fine weather.

Night navigation needs great care.

weather is encountered. Just how much extra allowance will be given to safe distances off hazards will be dependent on just how bad the weather is, how well the navigator knows the coast, and what sort of a coastline it is. Experience is the best guide.

Lee shore
Sail boats in particular, but power boats also, need to give a wide berth to a lee shore. This is the shore onto which the wind blows, and navigating too close can mean that in the event of an accident (lost mast, motor failure), the boat will blow ashore before emergency action can be taken.

Since it is hard to predict which will be the lee shore when planning the passage some days beforehand, this is another adjustment which may need to be made when actually under way along the course lines. The danger circle which covers a hazard to leeward should have a greater margin of safety than one to windward.

Night navigation
There is always less opportunity to keep a check on the boat's progress at night since many of the shore objects, and often even the shore itself, cannot be seen or can only be seen indistinctly. Safety allowances for hazards and dangers should therefore always be much greater at night than during the daytime.

Heavy weather

As with night navigation, visibility is often restricted in bad weather and precautions should be taken to ensure that safety margins are increased. Particularly is this the case since heavy weather can cause the boat to be buffeted off course very easily and make recovery very difficult.

Leeway

The drift caused by the wind is known as leeway. On a motor cruiser it may be fairly negligible, but on a yacht it is considerable. Indeed, leeway of up to 10° is not at all uncommon, and thus if the boat is to hold anything like an accurate course, it must be taken into consideration when planning the passage.

There is only one way to find the leeway affecting your boat, and that is by experience. It can in no way be calculated, other than perhaps by computer, and few navigators have one of those in their craft! By sailing directly for a shore mark, and noting the amount of drift to leeward the boat makes, a gradual idea of how much leeway she makes under differing conditions can be assessed.

The most difficult aspect of calculating leeway is the number of factors involved. Leeway is different, for example, when sailing on the wind to when sailing down wind. Similarly it will vary from the time that the boat is sailing upright to when she is lying on her lee gunwale. And every boat makes different leeway due to her different underwater area.

When a fair idea of leeway has been gained, it can be allowed when setting a course by adjusting the course to be steered allowing the leeway angle *into* the wind.

Calm weather can be almost as big a problem as heavy weather to a yacht!

There is little leeway made when running down wind.

Tides and currents

Currents and tidal streams create some of the biggest problems encountered on a coastal passage. A current runs consistently in the same direction, a tidal stream flows backwards and forwards, usually twice a day.

Currents are mostly associated with the oceans, but in some parts of the world, where they move close to the coast, they affect coastal navigation. Tidal streams are a feature of coastal waters and will be encountered in every estuary and harbour as well as some distance offshore.

Tidal stream charts are published for waters where tidal streams are strong or vary considerably in direction. These usually indicate the flow of tidal streams at hourly intervals before and after high water. Current charts are also published by the authorities, and information concerning both tidal and current charts can be obtained from the *Sailing Directions* or *Pilots*. When the direction and rate of flow of a current is known it can be counteracted as described in Chapter 7. But many tidal flows are irregular and many currents have eddies which swirl in all directions.

This means that the effects of tidal streams and currents on the boat often cannot be predicted, adding yet another factor to the problems facing the navigator when under way.

Latitude and longitude positions

Although the boat's position is rarely plotted in terms of latitude and longitude when making a coastal passage, it is

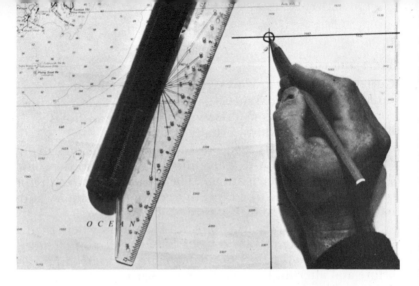

sometimes necessary to locate a position given in latitude and longitude on the chart. The procedure then is as follows:

1 Locate the latitude position on the left or right side of the chart and mark it with a pencil.
2 Place the parallel rules against the nearest parallel of latitude on the chart then run them down until one edge is touching the latitude marked. Draw a line across the chart.
3 Repeat the procedure using the longitude scale and the nearest meridian of longitude.
4 Where the two lines thus drawn intersect is the fix of the position.

It follows that by reversing this process the navigator can find the latitude and longitude of his own boat's position. Although not often used when coasting, other than in emergency conditions, latitude and longitude positions are usually entered in the log book as a record of the boat's progress during the passage.

DR position

The DR (dead reckoning) position of the boat is not a fix. It is the position arrived at by calculation using the boat's past courses and log distances. The usual method of finding the DR position when coasting is to mark off along the laid course line the distance run by log from the last known fix.

A DR position is marked with a triangle. The dot in the centre of the triangle marks the exact spot.

Chapter 6   Plotting the Track

Set and drift

Plotting is the means whereby the navigator keeps a track of the boat's progress. Once the course is laid and she begins her passage along it, a number of unknown factors will affect her and probably push her off the set course line.

These factors, some of which were described in the previous chapter, can include tidal effects, currents, wind and wave effect . . . in short, anything which the navigator does not know in advance and therefore has not allowed for. Even bad steering on the part of the helmsman can add to the factors setting the boat off course.

The sum total of all these unknown factors is termed *set*, and the distance it pushes the boat off course is termed *drift*. These terms are also used in connection with known currents and tidal flows in exactly the same context. The set of a current is the direction it pushes the boat. The drift is the distance it pushes her off course.

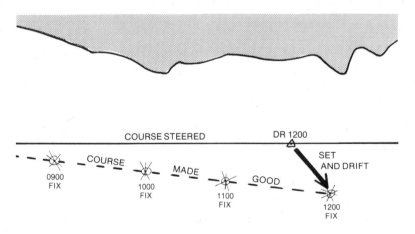

69

The timing of plots can be varied according to conditions, providing they give the navigator a clear picture of the track the boat is making and the forces affecting her.

Timing of plots

It follows, then, that if an unknown set is affecting the boat she will not follow the laid course line, but will be pushed either inshore or offshore. In practice a boat rarely keeps to her track and is affected by set on almost every course. Later we shall deal with the question of determining the amount of set and drift and allowing for it in our calculations. But initially the important thing is to keep track of what it is doing to the boat and ensure that she is not pushed into danger.

This is done by plotting her position at regular intervals. Just how regular depends on her location and the conditions at the time. Close inshore on a dangerous coastline, for example, it would be wise to make a plot every half hour. Well offshore or in clear weather, once an hour will suffice.

The fix

A fix is an exact plot of the boat's position determined by navigational means. Plotting the boat's track is done by means of a series of fixes, indicating her progress along the course line. Each costal fix is the result of taking compass bearing of shore objects. There are a number of different methods of obtaining a fix, each of which depends on the number and type of shore objects visible.

Laying off a bearing

In Chapter 3 we took a bearing of a shore object using the hand-bearing compass. By laying off (plotting) this bearing on the

chart we are well on the way to determining the boat's position, for if a bearing is correctly taken and laid off on the chart, then:

The position of the boat must lie somewhere along that bearing.

As described, the bearing is taken by sighting over the compass. It is then converted to true so that it can be laid off on the chart. The procedure for laying off is as follows:

1 Find the bearing on the circumference of the compass rose nearest the object.
2 Place the parallel rules so that one edge runs through the centre of the compass rose and also cuts the circumference at the bearing reading. (*above left*).
3 Carefully move the parallel rules across the chart until one edge touches the object from which the bearing was taken.
4 Draw a line along the edge of the rules to seaward of the object. This represents the bearing taken of the object, and the position of the boat must lie somewhere along this bearing. (*above right*).

Because the fix of the boat's position is made by use of these compass bearings, it follows that they must be taken with great care and accuracy. An error of one or two degrees can be magnified into even larger errors when used with certain fixes and give the navigator a completely false position.

It also follows that if the boat's position lies somewhere along a bearing, a basic fix of her position can be found by taking a bearing of another object at the same time. The boat must be located at the point where both bearings cross.

Typical objects for taking bearings

As mentioned, literally anything on shore that is readily visible from sea can be used for taking bearings. However, by virtue of their shape or location, some objects are better than others. A lighthouse, for example, since it is located right on the coastline, is painted white and is easily pinpointed, makes the ideal bearing object. A mountain, which may be situated way back from the coast, has no definite peak and may be lost or confused by inshore haze, is not good.

The cross bearing fix

This is the most commonly used form of fix, particularly in daytime, since it requires three shore objects to be readily visible at the same time. Ideally, these shore objects should be spaced out at angles of roughly 60°. The finer (or broader) the angle between each object, the less accurate the fix.

The type of object is not important providing it gives a good bearing and is easily identified on the chart. Two bearings can be used, but the margin for error is greater and three is accepted as offering the best fix. The procedure is as follows:

1 Select three shore objects well spaced and identify them on the chart. Take a bearing of each as quickly as possible.
2 Convert each bearing to true and measure the first against the compass rose.
3 Transfer the bearing through the shore object and lay it off on the chart.
4 Repeat the process with the second bearing.
5 And the third bearing.
6 Where all three bearings cross is the fix of the boat's position.

Cocked hat

It frequently happens in small boat navigation that the three bearings of a cross bearing fix do not cross exactly, but form a small triangle. This is known as a 'cocked hat'. Because of the difficulties in taking three quick bearings from a tossing boat, the cocked hat can be accepted as a fix providing the triangle so formed is not too large. A big cocked hat would be an indication of errors somewhere in the fix and the bearings should be taken again.

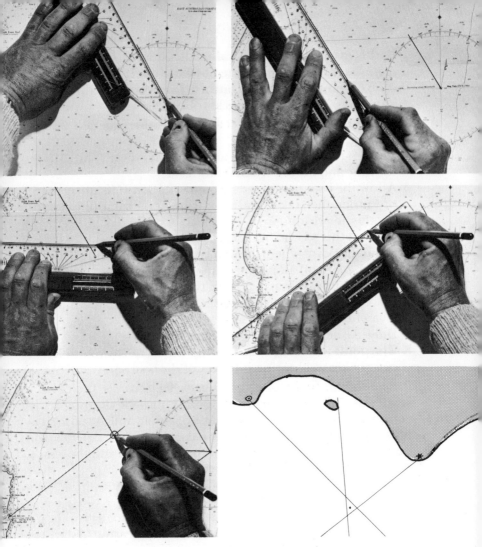

If for some reason it is not possible to retake the fix, the corner of the triangle closest to shore should be taken as the fix position. This affords a safety margin.

The running fix

It is not always possible to obtain three shore objects close enough to use for a cross bearing fix. Indeed, often there is only one suitable object visible, particularly at night when fixes can be made only with lights, and navigation lights are usually well spaced out.

In this case, the fix used is called the running fix, also sometimes called the transferred bearing fix. It again involves the use of compass bearings, but also requires the reading of the distance log. The procedure is as follows:

1 Take a bearing of the object and at the same time take the log reading.
2 Convert the bearing to true and lay it off on the chart. Mark the time and the log reading alongside.
3 Allow the boat to proceed on course for some distance, say 3 or 4 miles, then take another bearing of the same object and another log reading.
4 Convert this second bearing to true and lay off on the chart.
5 From the point where the first bearing and the course line intersect, mark off along the course line the distance run by log between the two bearings. Call this point X.
6 Place the parallel rules against the first bearing and transfer it carefully to point X.
7 Draw a line through X.
8 The point where the first bearing, transferred through X, cuts the second bearing is the fix of the boat's position.

Because this fix involves a run between bearings, there is a small possibility of error creeping in. Thus, one running fix is considered only a guide to the boat's position, and the process is repeated several times as the boat passes the object. After two or three running fixes, all errors will be eliminated and the boat's position will be established beyond doubt.

Running fix between two objects

Where two well spaced objects are not suitable for a cross bearing fix, the running fix may be adopted. The bearing of the first object is transferred the log distance run in just the same way as when using one object. Where it crosses the bearing of the second object is the fix of the boat's position.

The cross bearing fix with three shore objects, and the running fix when only one shore object is visible, are the basis on which plotting the boat's progress along her coastal passage is established. However, there are other useful fixes which can be used providing conditions are suitable and objects are available.

Stages in plotting
a running fix.

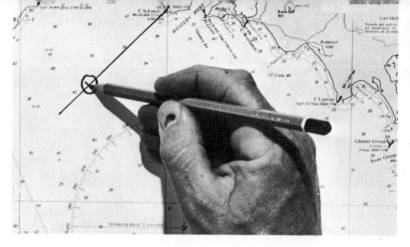

The extreme range fix

An excellent fix, used mostly at night when making a landfall,
or approaching a lighthouse from a long distance off. It
depends on clear weather and seeing the 'loom' of the light (see
Chapter 4). The procedure is as follows:

1 Watch the loom of the light. Identify the light on the chart.
2 When it 'breaks' take a bearing. Convert to true and lay off on
   the chart.
3 Enter the nautical tables in the *Extreme Range Table* with
   arguments height of eye of the navigator, and height of the
   light (from the chart). Take out the 'distance off' the light.
4 Measure it along the chart bearing.
5 The result is a fix of the boat's position.

Four point bearing fix

This is a handy rule-of-thumb fix which does not require the
use of compass or chart. It is ideal for checking the boat's position in clear weather and when all things are bearing an equal
strain. In short, it is a simple but effective check of the boat's
progress and whether or not she is being pushed inside or outside the course line by an unknown set.

The four point bearing is the bearing which is 45° to the
course on either side of the bow. Generally speaking, the points
of the compass are not used greatly nowadays. But with dead
ahead as zero, it was always accepted that the beam of the boat
(90° from ahead) was eight points on either side and the
intervening area was divided up into points of 11¼° each.

However, only the four point position, 45° on either side of

76

Although more accurate using a hand-bearing compass, the four point bearing fix can be obtained without any instruments other than the log.

the bow, is used in modern navigation, the remainder of the points having gone the way of the cardinal compass which gave rise to them.

A good navigator will know his four point bearing. From the cockpit position, a shroud, or ventilator, or stanchion, or even a mark on the gunwale will indicate the 45°, four point location. With this established, the procedure is as follows:

1 Watch the approach of the object until it is on the four point bearing. Read the log.
2 Allow the boat to continue along her course line until the object is on the beam bearing. Read the log again.
3 The distance travelled by log between the two bearings is equal to the distance off the object on the beam bearing. The conscientious navigator, knowing how far off the object he intended to pass, will thus know whether or not the boat is maintaining her course line.

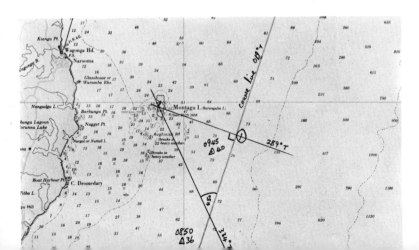

Doubling the angle on the bow

This is another handy check on the boat's progress, requiring the use of both compass and log. The procedure is as follows:

1 When the object is fine on the bow, take a compass bearing. Read the log.
2 Find the *relative bearing* (i.e. the angle on the bow) by adding or subtracting the bearing to the course line.
3 Allow the boat to continue on course until the relative bearing has doubled. Read the log.
4 The distance run by log between the two bearings is the distance off the object on the second bearing.
5 Convert the second bearing to true and lay off on the chart, marking off the distance run by log.
6 The result is a fix of the boat's position.

Fix by vertical sextant angle

This is perhaps the most accurate and easy fix to make when 'rock hopping', or running close in to the coastline. It requires the use of a sextant as well as the hand bearing compass, but is more accurate than any other fix and therefore ideal for plotting under close or difficult navigational conditions. Most experienced yachtsmen who use this fix prefer it even to the cross bearing or running fix when coasting close to the shore.

1 Take a bearing of the object, which needs to be reasonably high.
2 Take a sextant reading, bringing the top of the lighthouse (or object) down to sea level in the telescope.
3 Convert the bearing to true and lay off on the chart.
4 Enter the nautical tables in the *Distance by Sextant Angle* table, using the arguments of the height of the object, from

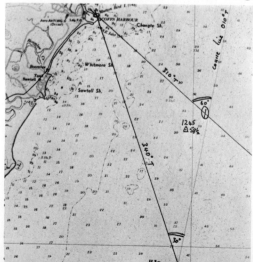

Doubling the angle on the bow.

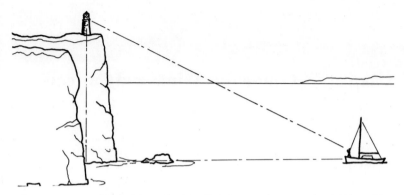

The sextant measures the angle of the lighthouse above sea level. The table converts this angle to a distance off the shore.

the chart and the angle measured on the sextant. The result will be the distance off the object.

5 Measure with the dividers the distance obtained from the table, along the bearing laid off on the chart.

6 The result is a fix of the boat's position.

Ad infinitum

There are, of course, many other ways of fixing the boat's position and keeping a check on her progress. Indeed, it depends only on the navigator's ingenuity as to the number and type of fixes which can be used. Those given in this chapter are the principal fixes used internationally for coastal navigation and cover the range of conditions which might normally be experienced aboard a small boat.

Chapter 7   **Countering Winds and Currents**

Set

As mentioned earlier, set is caused by a number of factors, some known and some unknown. Obviously, then, it can be allowed for in cases where its effect is known, but where it is composed of unknown factors its effect must first be found before action to counter it can be taken.

Countering a known set

When laying a course across a stretch of water which contains a known movement such as an ocean current or an established tidal flow, the navigator can take action to counter the effect of the set which will be experienced, and keep his boat on the planned course line. The procedure is as follows:

1 From the departure point, lay off a line representing in both direction and distance one hour of current. Call the terminal point X.
2 Set the dividers at a distance representing the number of miles the boat will travel in one hour without the effect of the current.

Close inshore, currents are usually tidal and predictable.

COURSE (TO MAKE GOOD)

Y

CURRENT (1 hr)

COURSE TO STEER BOAT (1 hr)

X

3 Place the point of the dividers on X and move them to intersect with the original course line at point Y.
4 Join X and Y. This line, when measured on the compass rose, is the course to steer to counteract the known current and maintain the original course line.
5 The distance along the course line from departure point to Y represents the distance the boat will travel in one hour while being affected by the current.

The one hour period is arbitrary, of course, and where the scale of the chart is small, two or more hours can be used, providing the same period is used throughout the calculation.

Countering an unknown set

This is much more difficult in practice because before countering the effect of the set, it must first be found. However, this is also the most common practice when coasting as rarely will the effect of set be known well enough to use the previous method.

The course made good

As the boat progresses along her course line, the set will tend to push her inshore or offshore from the course line. At first this will be a relatively small amount, but will be exaggerated as time passes to the point where she is too far off course and adjustments must be made to bring her back to her original destination.

Since plotting is carried out at frequent intervals, a series of fixes on the chart will show the amount and direction the boat has set off course. If these plots are joined by a line from the departure point (or last known fix on the course line) the track

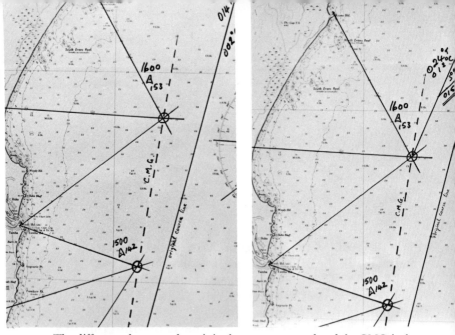

The difference between the original course as steered and the CMG is the set experienced (3 degrees). The new course is relaid from the last fix at 1600 to the destination (024 T), compass error applied (12°E), leaving a compass course of 012 C. The set is then applied in the opposite direction to its effect (+3); the resultant new course to steer allowing for the set and making 024 T is 015 C. *(above right)*

she has made under the influence of the unknown set can be seen. This is known as the Course Made Good (CMG) and can be measured on the compass rose.

The angle of set

If the boat has been steering one course and making good another, then obviously the difference between them is the effect of the unknown set. It is measured as an angle simply by subtracting the course steered from the course made good (or vice versa) and is termed the angle of set.

Correcting the course

By the time the angle of set has been established, the boat will have been pushed well off course. Thus a new course must be laid off from the last fix to the destination or arrival point. This is measured on the compass rose and must be converted to compass before altering to steer along that line. However, while this new course will head the boat back to her original destination

82

there is still the set to take into consideration and this is done by applying the *angle of set* against the direction of the current.

Unfortunately, this newly found set is likely to change as the boat proceeds along her course line, for rarely does it remain constant for very long. By continuing to plot the boat's progress with a series of fixes at regular intervals, the picture of what is happening to her as a result of the changing set becomes apparent, and adjustments can be made to keep her travelling along the original course line.

In practice it is often unnecessary to re-lay the course and find the angle of set each time the boat digresses from her set course line. By making small adjustments to the amount of set previously allowed, the smart navigator can keep her pretty well on her planned course the whole time, and he will simply instruct the helmsman to add or subtract a degree or two from the course steered.

Leeway

As described in Chapter 5, leeway is another of the great unknowns as far as navigation is concerned. However, it can be determined with reasonable accuracy during the course of sailing the boat, and the angle of leeway can be measured and applied to the course steered in much the same way as the angle of set.

The only real way to find leeway is to sail the boat under all conditions and rigs, remembering that even one sail change can affect the leeway, as can the amount of heel and the angle to the wind at which she is sailing. The procedure, to be repeated under all these differing conditions, is roughly as follows:

1 Establish a buoy or similar mark in the water as the starting point. Determine the compass course to steer from this point to another buoy or shore object, by laying it off on the chart then applying compass error.
2 From the starting point, sail the boat along this course, *steering by compass.*
3 As the boat progresses, take a quick series of fixes to establish her course made good on the chart.
4 The difference between the course steered and the CMG will be the leeway under the existing conditions.
5 Repeat with different weather and sail conditions until

Leeway should be found and
checked as described before leaving
port.

satisfied that you have established the boat's leeway on all
points.

Note: It goes without saying that this method will only be
accurate if carried out when there is no tidal or current movement. The safest system is to make a number of runs along the
course at tidal slack water (high or low tide) in an area where
tidal movement is accurately predictable.

It also goes without saying that to build up an accurate picture of the boat's leeway is a job that will take some time in
order to encompass all the different points of sailing and
different wind conditions. By using a little ingenuity, however,
the navigator will find many opportunities during normal sailing, and particularly during racing, to use this method to check
leeway affecting the boat.

Applying leeway

As with set, having found leeway, it is easy to apply. The leeway
angle is simply added or subtracted from the steered course by
applying it *into* the wind.

Tack navigation

So far we have laid off courses, plotted and allowed for set and
leeway assuming always that the boat can progress directly in
any direction. With a motor cruiser this is always the case, but
yachts cannot sail directly into the wind and are thus handi-
capped when making a course in that direction.

A fairly average angle of approach to the wind with cruising
yachts is around 45°. This means that there is a 90° zone, (45° on
either side of the wind) in which she cannot sail. If the course to
be steered is in that zone, then the boat must tack at the 45°

angle to the wind on either side of it, using it as a 'mean' course by which to judge the length of the tacks.

If every boat sailed at exactly 45° to the wind, the navigational aspect would be fairly simple, but some boats 'point' higher into the wind than others, and then again, some point higher on one tack than another. What this means, in effect, is that the actual course that the boat will steer on her tack cannot be plotted ahead if she is to use best advantage of the wind and sail on her best windward course. The procedure for tack navigation, then, is as follows:

1 Set the boat on her first tack, watching the sails to get her best sailing position. When she has settled down on this tack, note the course on the compass.

2 Convert this course to true by applying compass error, and *take off the leeway* by applying it in the opposite direction to that used when putting it on (i.e. apply it in the direction the wind is blowing).

3 Lay this course off on the chart. This is the track she will make providing the wind does not change.

4 At a predetermined point, put the boat onto the other tack and repeat the procedure.

5 Allow her to run back over the laid course line, then at a predetermined distance on the other side, put her about again. Repeat the procedure in such a way that her mean course into the wind is the course laid off on the chart.

If set has been allowed, it must be removed in the same way as leeway before plotting the tack course on the chart. Fixes should be taken continuously to check on the progress of the boat and adjustments made as they become obvious.

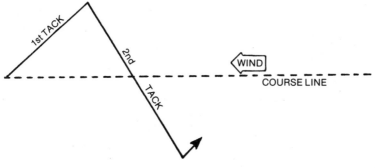

Chapter 8   Tides and Tidal Streams

Tidal stream charts

Many coastlines of the world have a simple ebb and flow of tide with a moderate rise and fall, and relatively insignificant tidal streams. However, many estuaries and land-locked coastal waters are affected by strong tidal streams which can make navigation very difficult. Not only does the speed of the flow vary at different stages of the tide, but the direction of the flow can swirl in eddies and create enormous problems for navigators unless they are familiar with the area.

Tidal stream charts available show the direction of tidal streams usually at hourly intervals before and after high water at the standard port for the area. Thus to learn of the direction and speed of tidal flow, the navigator should plot his position at the hourly intervals of the charts and determine the tidal problems he may expect. Where tidal streams are less complicated, tidal stream charts may provide one chart indicating the movements of the flood stream and one indicating the ebb.

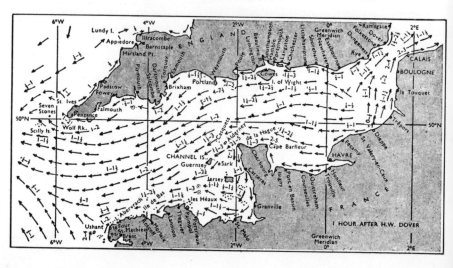

Ocean currents

Although primarily concerned with ocean navigation, when ocean currents skirt a coastline they have a considerable effect on coastal navigation. Typical examples are the Aghullas current east of South Africa, and the East Australian current, which affects shipping navigating the East Coast of Australia from Sydney north. Fortunately these currents are well charted in terms of direction and speed and, since they flow consistently in the one direction, their effects are easily predicted.

Tides

Tides are caused by a massive tidal wave that moves across the world constantly. Since some 75 per cent of the earth's surface is covered by salt water, this huge movement of the oceans affects literally every corner of every coastline in the world. As the wave reaches a coastline it creates a rise in the water levels of estuaries and harbours. As it moves on, the water level drops thus creating the tidal cycle as we know it.

Effect of sun and moon

The cause of tides is principally the gravitational effect of the sun and moon, the latter, being closer to earth, creating the stronger pull. This gravitational pull tends to draw the water around the earth's surface into a wave formation, and the rotation of the globe in effect moves this wave around its surface.

It follows that if the sun and moon are pulling in the same direction they will pile up a very high tidal wave and when pulling across each other, a relatively low wave. Because this wave builds up on either side of the world, the greatest pull of sun and moon is when they are on the same side of earth or on

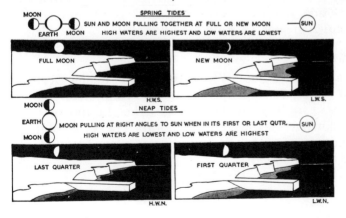

Tidal currents are felt most at the narrow entrances to waterways.

Tides can win or lose a race and are thus vitally important to high performance racing yachts.

diametrically opposite sides. The time when their respective pull is negated by one another is when they are pulling at right angles.

Thus, twice a month, at new moon (sun on the same side) and full moon (sun on the opposite side of earth), this high tidal wave is built up. It is termed a *spring tide*. When the sun and moon are at right angles in the first and third quarter, the lower tidal waves create what are known as *neap tides*.

Spring tides

For the navigator, the effect of the tides comes in two forms—the rush of water created by the tidal flow, and the depth of water over the sea bed created by the rising and falling tide. Since spring tides are caused by the higher tidal wave everything is exaggerated, so that the tidal flow is faster and the depths are greater than normal at high tide and less than normal at low tide. While the period of the tide is the same, its range is much greater, i.e. *high high tides and low low tides*.

Neap tides

These are the 'quiet' tides. With a much lower tidal wave, the inrush of water is less and thus the tidal flow slower. High tides are average or slightly less than average in height, and low tides are never down to the lowest of the month. The period of the tide is again the same, but the range is much less, i.e. *low high tides and high low tides*.

The depth of water over a dangerous bar is of utmost importance to the navigator. Chart datum indicates the least depth.

Chart datum

The soundings marked on a chart are taken at the lowest tide of the month, and therefore there is *almost never* less water over the sea bottom than that marked on the chart. This level is termed chart datum and tide heights are recorded above it, so to find the depth of water over the sea bed at a given time:

the height of the tide from the tide tables is added to the depth of water on the chart.

Tidal anomalies

One of the most unsettling factors about tides is their habit of doing the unexpected thing at an unexpected time. Due to the topography of the sea bottom, it is not unusual for some ports to have an outgoing tide when the tide should be flooding and vice versa. In other ports a rise and fall (range) of tide of 40 feet may be experienced, creating all kinds of problems in the maritime scene. And to make life even more difficult, some ports have four high and four low tides a day!

With the exception of northern coastlines, Australian waters are fairly free of these anomalies.

Tide tables

Official tide tables are computed by the hydrographic office and these are the only ones that should be used for navigation. Other tide tables, particularly commercial ones, *may* be quite accurate, but some are not, and the risk is too great when navigating a boat in shallow waters, for the time and height of the tide may be the difference between a safe passage and running aground.

89

Tide tables are drawn up for standard ports and secondary ports. In the former case, the tide times and heights are for a specific port, usually a principal commercial port and can simply be read off like any other table.

Secondary ports, by contrast, merely have an adjustment of time and height to be applied to the nearest listed standard port and do not have their own tides listed for each hour of the day. However, application of the adjustment is quite straightforward and requires no great mental effort.

Using the tide tables

Standard port

Assume that we are working on the tide tables of which an excerpt is included here. The port is Sydney. Let's find the depth of water over a shoal patch marked on the chart as having a 1 fathom 3 feet sounding. The date is 4 July and the time 4am.

Chart sounding	9.0 ft
Height of tide at 0400	1.0 ft
Depth of water over shoal	**10.0 ft**

AUSTRALIA, EAST COAST — SYDNEY (FORT DENISON)
Lat. 33° 51' S. Long. 151° 14' E.

TIME ZONE: –1000 — TIMES AND HEIGHTS OF HIGH AND LOW WATERS — YEAR: 1966

MAY

Day	Time	Ht. Ft.	Time	Ht. Ft.		Day	Time	Ht. Ft.	Time	Ht. Ft.
1 Su	0504	5·3	1138	0·8		16 M	0515	4·6	1136	1·4
	1752	4·8	2348	1·2			1800	4·7	2359	1·8
2 M	0602	5·3	1224	0·6		17 Tu	0559	4·6	1212	1·3
	1841	5·2					1837	5·0		
3 Tu	0046	0·9	0656	5·2		18 W	0045	1·6	0645	4·6
	1307	0·6	1925	5·4			1247	1·2	1914	5·3
4 W	0142	0·6	0746	5·0		19 Th	0130	1·4	0731	4·5
	1348	0·6	2008	5·8			1322	1·2	1950	5·6
5 Th	0233	0·5	0834	4·8		20 F	0214	1·1	0812	4·3
	1427	0·8	2050	5·8			1359	1·3	2026	5·8
6 F	0323	0·5	0920	4·5		21 Sa	0256	0·9	0856	4·1
	1506	1·1	2130	5·6			1436	1·4	2104	6·0
7 Sa	0412	0·6	1006	4·2		22 Su	0344	0·8	0941	4·1
	1545	1·4	2212	5·8			1516	1·5	2145	6·1
8 Su	0459	0·9	1054	4·0		23 M	0431	0·9	1030	4·3
	1625	1·7	2256	5·6			1600	1·8	2230	6·0
9 M	0549	1·1	1145	3·8		24 Tu	0522	0·9	1124	1·8
	1709	2·0	2341	5·3			1649	1·8	1823	2·3
10 Tu	0641	1·4	1243	3·7		25 W	0617	1·0	1220	4·1
	1759	2·3					1745	1·9		
11 W	0054	5·1	0737	1·7		26 Th	0018	5·1	0718	1·1
	1345	3·7	1900	2·5			1325	4·2	1851	2·0
12 Th	0133	4·7	0836	1·8		27 F	0121	5·5	0820	1·1
	1446	3·8	2011	2·5			1433	4·1	2006	2·0
13 F	0234	4·7	0951	1·9		28 Sa	0228	5·3	0921	0·9
	1544	3·9	2119	2·3			1537	4·1	2123	1·8
14 Sa	0333	4·6	1017	1·9		29 Su	0336	5·1	1015	0·9
	1636	3·9	2218	2·3			1636	4·7	2234	1·6
15 Su	0425	4·5	1059	1·5		30 M	0441	4·8	1119	1·6
	1719	4·0	2310	2·1			1729	5·0	2340	1·3
						31 Tu	0542	4·7	1148	0·9
							1818	5·4		

JUNE

Day	Time	Ht. Ft.	Time	Ht. Ft.		Day	Time	Ht. Ft.	Time	Ht. Ft.
1 W	0040	1·0	0658	4·5		16 Th	0017	1·7	0610	4·2
	1232	1·0	1903	5·7			1200	1·4	1859	5·5
2 Th	0136	0·8	0731	4·5		17 F	0107	1·3	0703	4·3
	1314	1·1	1946	5·7			1242	1·3	1920	5·8
3 F	0227	0·7	0819	4·2		18 Sa	0156	1·0	0752	4·3
	1356	1·2	2028	6·0			1327	1·3	2002	6·1
4 Sa	0315	0·7	0906	4·0		19 Su	0245	0·8	0841	4·3
	1437	1·4	2109	5·9			1413	1·3	2047	6·2
5 Su	0359	0·8	0950	3·9		20 M	0332	0·6	0930	4·3
	1519	1·6	2150	5·8			1501	1·3	2131	6·3
6 M	0442	0·9	1035	3·8		21 Tu	0421	0·5	1020	4·3
	1601	1·8	2231	5·6			1551	1·3	2220	6·3
7 Tu	0525	1·1	1120	3·8		22 W	0511	0·5	1111	4·5
	1645	1·9	2315	5·4			1643	1·4	2311	6·1
8 W	0610	1·3	1208	3·8		23 Th	0602	0·6	1204	4·5
	1731	2·1					1739	1·5		
9 Th	0000	5·1	0656	1·5		24 F	0005	5·8	0657	0·7
	1301	3·8	1823	2·3			1305	4·5	1842	1·6
10 F	0049	4·9	0744	1·6		25 Sa	0100	5·4	0744	1·0
	1357	3·9	1922	2·4			1406	4·6	1954	1·7
11 Sa	0138	4·7	0833	1·7		26 Su	0205	5·0	0833	1·2
	1456	4·1	2027	2·4			1509	4·6	2057	1·8
12 Su	0231	4·6	0918	1·6		27 M	0259	4·6	0920	1·3
	1554	4·2	2131	2·1			1610	4·9	2226	1·5
13 M	0324	4·4	1000	1·4		28 Tu	0419	4·3	1030	1·3
	1651	4·4	2229	1·8			1705	5·2	2335	1·3
14 Tu	0415	4·3	1040	1·3		29 W	0527	4·3	1117	1·2
	1745	4·7	2325	1·4			1757	5·4		
15 W	0505	4·3	1119	1·1		30 Th	0038	1·1	0627	4·4
	1837	5·0					1156	1·1	1845	5·6

JULY

Day	Time	Ht. Ft.	Time	Ht. Ft.		Day	Time	Ht. Ft.	Time	Ht. Ft.
1 F	0132	0·9	0723	3·8		16 Sa	0045	1·2	0641	4·0
	1248	1·4	1929	5·7			1212	1·4	1856	5·9
2 Sa	0220	0·9	0810	3·8		17 Su	0138	0·9	0754	4·2
	1333	1·5	2011	5·8			1306	1·4	1943	6·2
3 Su	0303	0·8	0851	3·8		18 M	0227	0·5	0825	4·5
	1417	1·5	2052	5·7			1357	1·0	2031	6·4
4 M	0342	0·9	0930	3·9		19 Tu	0315	0·3	0913	4·5
	1500	1·5	2130	5·7			1449	0·9	2119	6·4
5 Tu	0419	0·9	1009	3·9		20 W	0401	0·2	0959	4·5
	1540	1·6	2209	5·5			1539	0·8	2207	6·3
6 W	0456	1·0	1049	3·9		21 Th	0450	0·2	1050	4·5
	1620	1·7	2248	5·3			1632	0·9	2257	6·1
7 Th	0533	1·2	1130	3·9		22 F	0537	0·5	1142	4·6
	1702	1·8	2325	5·1			1728	1·0	2347	5·7
8 F	0611	1·3	1216	3·9		23 Sa	0626	0·5	1237	4·6
	1745	2·0					1829	1·3		
9 Sa	0004	4·9	0650	1·4		24 Su	0044	5·1	0716	0·7
	1304	3·9	1835	2·2			1338	4·7	1940	1·5
10 Su	0046	4·7	0731	1·5		25 M	0145	4·7	0809	1·0
	1355	4·1	1933	2·3			1442	5·0	2100	1·6
11 M	0134	4·4	0814	1·4		26 Tu	0243	4·3	0901	1·2
	1450	4·2	2041	2·1			1546	5·2	2218	1·5
12 Tu	0250	4·2	0858	1·4		27 W	0409	3·8	1000	1·5
	1538	4·6	2149	2·2			1645	5·5	2332	1·3
13 W	0352	4·0	0928	1·2		28 Th	0522	3·6	1056	1·4
	1628	4·9	2252	2·0			1730	5·3		
14 Th	0451	4·0	1040	1·0		29 F	0033	1·2	0621	3·8
	1718	5·2	2335	1·3			1146	1·6	1730	5·4
15 F	0544	3·9	1121	1·5		30 Sa	0112	1·0	0713	3·7
	1807	5·5					1221	1·5	1915	5·5
						31 Su	0205	0·6	0754	3·7
							1320	1·5	1955	5·5

AUGUST

Day	Time	Ht. Ft.	Time	Ht. Ft.		Day	Time	Ht. Ft.	Time	Ht. Ft.
1 M	0242	0·9	0830	3·8		16 Tu	0206	0·3	0804	4·5
	1343	1·5	2033	5·5			1343	0·6	2015	6·3
2 Tu	0316	0·9	0905	3·9		17 W	0252	0·0	0850	4·7
	1442	1·3	2109	5·5			1435	0·4	2102	6·4
3 W	0349	0·9	0939	4·0		18 Th	0337	–0·1	0937	4·8
	1519	1·3	2145	5·4			1527	0·3	2149	6·2
4 Th	0420	0·9	1014	4·1		19 F	0421	0·0	1024	4·9
	1556	1·3	2217	5·2			1619	0·4	2237	5·8
5 F	0452	1·0	1051	4·1		20 Sa	0505	0·2	1112	4·9
	1633	1·5	2249	5·0			1715	0·7	2327	5·3
6 Sa	0524	1·1	1129	4·2		21 Su	0549	0·5	1206	4·9
	1712	1·6	2324	4·8			1816	1·0		
7 Su	0556	1·3	1209	4·2		22 M	0022	4·7	0637	0·9
	1757	1·9					1302	4·9	1924	1·3
8 M	0003	4·5	0630	1·6		23 Tu	0126	4·1	0728	1·2
	1256	4·2	1851	2·1			1406	4·9	2048	1·5
9 Tu	0108	4·0	0708	1·6		24 W	0212	3·7	0830	1·7
	1354	4·4	1958	2·2			1513	5·0	2209	1·5
10 W	0144	3·9	0756	1·5		25 Th	0403	3·5	0957	1·9
	1442	4·6	2113	2·0			1615	5·2	2320	1·3
11 Th	0255	3·7	0853	1·3		26 F	0518	3·5	1059	1·9
	1543	4·9	2225	1·9			1721	5·0		
12 F	0411	3·4	0955	1·8		27 Sa	0017	1·2	0614	3·6
	1644	5·1	2329	1·5			1135	1·8	1813	5·1
13 Sa	0525	3·8	1056	1·4		28 Su	0105	0·9	0655	3·7
	1741	5·5					1225	1·6	1856	5·2
14 Su	0025	1·1	0616	4·0		29 M	0153	0·5	0741	3·9
	1154	1·3	1935	5·8			1305	1·4	1935	5·3
15 M	0117	0·6	0716	4·2		30 Tu	0211	0·9	0834	4·2
	1249	0·9	1926	6·1			1344	1·0	2008	5·3
						31 W	0241	0·0	0834	4·2
							1421	1·1	2041	5·3

Excerpt from tide tables (standard port).

No.	PLACE	POSITION		TIME DIFFERENCES		MEAN HEIGHTS (IN FEET)				Reference
	STANDARD PORT	Lat.	Long.			HHW	LHW	LLW	HLW	
6037	SYDNEY	see page 95		HHW	LLW	5·2	4·2	1·0	1·4	
	SECONDARY PORTS	S.	E.	h. m.	h. m.	HEIGHT DIFFERENCES				
	Australia, east coast			(Zone −1000)						
6017	N.W. Solitary island . .	30°01′	153°17′	+0002	−0003	−0·2	−0·2	+0·4	+0·2	
6018	Coffs harbour . . .	30 18	153 09	−0015	−0015	+0·1	−0·1	+0·2	−0·1	
6020	Macleay river bar . .	30 53	153 02	+0013	+0011	−0·3	−0·3	+0·2	−0·2	
6022	Port Macquarie bar . .	31 26	152 56	+0012	+0011	−0·3	−0·3	+0·2	−0·2	
6024	Harrington inlet . . .	31 53	152 43	+0011	+0011	−0·3	−0·3	+0·1	−0·2	
6027	Broughton island . .	32 37	152 20	−0008	−0007	−0·4	−0·2	−0·4	0·0	
	Port Stephens									
6029	Nelson's bay . . .	32 43	152 09	+0016	+0017	+0·2	+0·2	+0·3	+0·3	
6030	Salamander bay . .	32 44	152 06	+0052	+0057	−0·1	−0·5	−0·4	−0·5	
6031	NEWCASTLE . . .	32 56	151 47	STANDARD PORT;		see page 92				
	Broken bay									
6034	Pittwater . . .	33 36	151 18	+0016	+0015	−0·2	−0·1	0·0	0·0	
	Port Jackson									
6036	Camp cove . . .	33 50	151 17	+0006	+0006	−0·1	−0·1	0·0	−0·1	
6037	SYDNEY (Fort Denison) .	33 51	151 14	STANDARD PORT						
6039	Botany bay . . .	34 01	151 08	+0022	+0023	−0·6	−0·5	−0·4	−0·4	
6042	Port Kembla . . .	34 29	150 55	0000	0000	−0·4	−0·2	−0·1	−0·3	
6044	Jervis bay . . .	35 07	150 44	−0006	−0002	−0·3	−0·2	−0·1	+0·1	
6046	Ulladulla harbour . .	35 22	150 30	−0003	+0001	−0·5	−0·4	0·0	−0·1	a
6048	Moruya river bar . .	35 54	150 08	+0010	+0010	−0·1	−0·5	+0·1	0·0	a
6050	Bermagui bar . . .	36 25	150 05	−0003	+0004	−0·3	−0·3	+0·4	+0·3	a
6053	Eden	37 04	149 54	0000	0000	−0·8	−0·6	−0·3	+0·1	t
6055	Gabo island . . .	37 34	149 55	−0010	−0001	+0·3	+0·3	+1·2	+1·2	a

No.	PLACE	POSITION	TIME DIFFERENCES		HWS	HWN	LWS	LWN	Reference
6093	MERSEY RIVER . . .	see page 104	MHW	MLW	9·7	8·8	1·0	1·9	
	BASS STRAIT								
6061	Rabbit island . . .	38 55 146 31	+0015	+0015	−2·7	−2·6	0·0	−0·1	a
	Kent group								
6063	Winter cove . . .	39 28 147 21	−0020	−0020	−1·7	−1·8	0·0	+0·1	a
6065	Great Glennie island . .	39 05 146 14	−0010	−0010	−1·8	−1·7	+0·1	0·0	a

No.	PLACE	POSITION	TIME DIFFERENCES		HHW	LHW	LLW	HLW	Reference
6073	PORT PHILLIP HEADS .	see page 98	HHW	LLW	4·7	4·3	1·0	1·9	
6067	Waratah bay . . .	38 52 146 00	−0005	+0005	+3·3	+3·3	+0·5	+1·0	
6068	Venus bay . . .	38 40 145 44	0000	◈	+2·3	+2·2	◈	◈	
	Westernport								
6069	Woody point . . .	38 31 145 22	÷0040	◈	+2·1	+1·9	◈	◈	a
6070	Mussel rock . . .	38 27 145 15	+0025	−0010	+4·2	+4·0	+0·9	+1·5	a
6071	Stony point . . .	38 22 145 13	+0045	+0010	+4·2	+4·0	+0·9	+1·4	t
	Port Phillip								
6073	HEADS, POINT LONS-DALE . . .	38 18 144 37	STANDARD PORT						
6074	Queenscliff . . .	38 19 144 40	+0024	◈	−0·7	◈	◈	◈	a

No.	PLACE	POSITION	TIME DIFFERENCES		HHW	LHW	LLW	HLW	Reference
6078	WILLIAMSTOWN . . .	see page 101	HHW	LLW	2·6	2·4	0·6	1·2	
6075	Schnapper point . .	38 13 145 02	−0025	◈	+0·2	◈	◈	◈	
6077	Geelong . . .	38 09 144 22	−0015	−0020	+0·1	+0·1	−0·2	+0·1	
6078	WILLIAMSTOWN, MEL-BOURNE . . .	37 52 144 52	STANDARD PORT						

Excerpt from tide tables (secondary port).

Secondary port

The date is still 4 July. The port is Coffs Harbour. We wish to find the time of high water (morning) at this port and the depth of water at that time over the bar which shows a sounding of 2 fathoms on the chart.

Time of am high tide, standard port (Sydney)	0930
Adjustment for secondary port (Coffs Harbour)	−0015
Time of high tide at Coffs Harbour	0915

Chart sounding   12.0 ft

Standard port high tide (depth) 3.9 ft
Secondary port adjustment   −0.1 ft
Secondary port high tide depth 3.8 ft   3.8 ft

Depth over bar at high tide   15.8 ft

Chapter 9 Harbour Pilotage

The IALA 'A' system of buoyage

This is new system of buoyage which has been introduced into British and European waters in recent years and is gradually being adopted in other parts of the world. It comprises two basic buoyage systems—Cardinal and Lateral—which are often used together to guide vessels through channels and around hazards.

The Cardinal system

This system uses a series of yellow and black painted buoys to indicate the compass direction of a danger or a point of interest. The colour pattern, as well as a specific topmark and light characteristic on the buoy indicates that it lies in the northern, eastern, western or southern quadrant of the compass when observed from the hazard. Thus observing, say, a yellow buoy with a black top and distinctive topmark, the navigator knows the danger lies to the south of this buoy. This system is in use in most parts of the world, usually in conjunction with the lateral system of buoyage.

The Lateral system

This system is somewhat similar to the old uniform lateral system of buoyage which existed in most parts of the world before introduction of the IALA systems. It consists mainly of red and green buoys or marks indicating, respectively, the port and starboard sides of a channel. The port hand markers are usually can-shaped and the starboard hand conical, with can and triangular topmarks respectively. These buoys must be kept on the side of the boat indicated when she is proceeding in from sea. Obviously, they are reversed when putting out to sea.

IALA BUOYAGE SYSTEM 'A'

LATERAL MARKS

PORT HAND

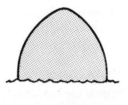

STARBOARD HAND

CARDINAL MARKS

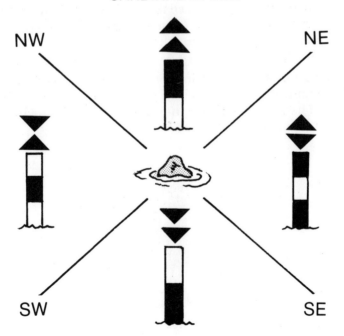

Other buoys

Different colours, shapes and topmarks are used with buoys to indicate special dangers or areas. These are detailed, as is all information about buoyage systems, in nautical almanacs such as Reeds.

Leaving harbour

It follows that since the colours, shapes and topmarks for buoys are related to the side of the boat on which they must be passed when *entering* harbour from seaward, these must be passed on the *opposite* side of the boat when leaving harbour for sea.

Harbour charts

A large scale harbour chart is essential before entering any port. These may be drawn as full charts (in big commercial harbours there may be a number of charts covering one harbour area) or just as plans, with a number of small ports included on the one chart (see Chapter 1).

Details, abbreviations and symbols on these are identical to other charts, the light characteristics of the buoys and marks being written as for larger, coastal lights, and the colour of the buoys indicated by the capital letter:

B—Black   R—Red   BW—Black and White

The use of the chart is vital, not only from the point of view of determining the best channel or the location of any unmarked hazards, but also to interpret the situation relating to danger or other special buoys.

SIGNALS FOR PASSING MOORED DREDGES

Day

To be shown so as to be visible all round

Night

Directions.—Pass Dredger on side Signals are exhibited. The passing vessel will keep Dredger on its starboard hand when entering harbour and on port hand when leaving harbour.

Fog Signal.—Morse Sound Signal Letter "A" made with dredger's bell.

Excerpt from *Sailing Directions* indicating dredge signals.

Sailing directions

As with the chart, consultation with the *Sailing Directions* is vital when entering a strange harbour. Information relating to all buoys, marks and channels is contained in this volume plus other vital details such as tidal movements, port signals and navigational information such as bridge heights or prohibited areas.

Dredge signals

Most commercial ports have dredges working somewhere and since these vessels almost invariably work in the channels it is important to be able to identify them and their signals indicating which side they may be passed. There is no system of marking which is adopted internationally, so the *Sailing Directions* or any published *Port Directions* must be studied to ensure that the navigator will identify a dredge (particularly at night) and know on which side it must be passed.

Port closed signals

Many ports, particularly smaller harbours and estuaries subject to bar conditions, may close the port to entering traffic if conditions necessitate this. Once again, the *Sailing Directions* will offer full details of the signals shown and where they are displayed. This information will not be found on the chart.

Weather signals

Like port closed signals, these are displayed from a prominent position and details of the signals and what they indicate will be found in the *Sailing Directions*.

Lead marks

These are described in detail in Chapter 4. By day, the usual system is triangular marks which must be lined up to enter the main channel. They are often painted with bright fluorescent colours so that they can be clearly seen even in poor visibility, and are replaced by lights at night. In small ports where a bar may be encountered, the marks may be moved as the channel changes so that they always represent the deepest or best channel for entry.

Piles and beacons

Smaller ports, non-commercial harbours and upper reaches of rivers may use piles or beacons instead of buoys to mark channels and hazards. The colour code and the shape of the topmark usually follows the uniform lateral code but once again this should be checked on the chart. The usual system is as follows:

Green pile, green triangular topmark—pass on the starboard side of the boat.

Red pile, red rectangular topmark—pass on the port side of the boat.

Since in upper reaches of rivers or estuaries it is sometimes difficult to ascertain which way represents seaward, the safest method of interpreting these marks is to always pass on the side the topmark is pointing.

Signal stations

Most harbours of any note have a signal station near the entrance which can be called by signal lamp and asked for information. The location of these signal stations and any special features about times of operating can be found in the *Sailing Directions*.

Pilots

Although pilots are available at many estuaries, they are rarely compulsory for yachts and small craft. However, it is always a wise precaution, both from the point of view of information relating to entering the port, and the possibility of navigational problems, to phone the Pilot Station or Port Officer before leaving the last departure port. This can save problems, particularly in bad weather, such as finding the port closed on arrival.

Anchorages

Suitable anchorages and sheltered spots are indicated in the *Sailing Directions* and sometimes on the chart. Offshore, their position is usually determined by the shelter they afford from the prevailing bad weather winds. In harbours they indicate the best location for both shelter and convenience.

Submarine cables

Most harbours have submarine cables running across the sea bed. Anchorage is strictly prohibited near these for obvious reasons, and they are clearly marked, usually with a large sign on the shore, and with a purple symbol on the chart.

Overhead cables

These can also create hazards for tall-masted yachts proceeding up a river or estuary. They are indicated on the chart and in the *Sailing Directions*.

Commercial shipping

Because they must stick rigidly to the dredged channels, freighters and other commercial or naval ships have right of way over yachts and motor cruisers within the limits of most major harbours. If there is sufficient water outside the channel, small craft should keep just clear of the marker buoys when encountering such traffic. Failing this, they must hug the *starboard* side of the channel until past and clear. It goes without saying that anchorage is prohibited in such channels.

Yacht races

Entering a popular waterway on a summer Saturday afternoon is somewhat akin to walking into a forest! Yacht races cover much of the water, and while the normal international rules for prevention of collision still prevail, it is common courtesy to avoid interfering with races unless absolutely necessary.

Special rules

Every port, particularly a big commercial port, has its own special rules concerning not only navigation, but the question of right of way. In many busy ports important vessels such as hovercraft and ferries have a special right of way over all pleasure craft. Such details can again be found in the *Sailing Directions* or *Port Rules*.

Speed limits

Almost every harbour has speed limits, and while these would apply only to fast power boats, their location should be known as the speed limit signs on the shore are not always obvious. Details of speed limits, as with all navigational details, are contained in the *Sailing Directions* or the *Port Rules*.

Crossing a bar

Most small harbours and river entrances have a bar across them, and since these can change quickly in both depth and the location of the channel, they present a formidable navigational hazard. Unfortunately, no two bars are the same, and information relating to each must be obtained from the local authorities in order to ensure safe navigation when entering.

It goes without saying that the condition of a bar deteriorates rapidly with bad seas or inclement weather conditions. The breaking waves on a bar are difficult to see when approached from seaward, and many a seaworthy craft has been lost by attempting to enter what appeared to be a relatively safe estuary. The Port Officer is the only person who can safely advise on bar conditions and, when planning to visit such a port, a telephone call to this official before leaving the last port can pay dividends.

Chapter 10 Weather and Weather Forecasting

Local weather conditions affect all sailors, not only the offshore navigator.

There is neither space nor justification in a book of this type for an in-depth study of weather systems and weather forecasting. The Bureau of Meteorology does a first-class job of interpreting and forecasting the weather and its predictions are readily available to boat owners through the telephone and the media.

However, in assessing the weather patterns and making their forecast, the Bureau of Meteorology of necessity covers a large area, often a whole state. And while the forecast over such an area may be generally correct, unexpected local developments can take place which can give rise to unpleasant conditions in one small area. Such local phenomena are almost impossible for the Bureau to forecast.

For the yachtsman offshore, however, the general weather pattern across the state is of interest only in indicating what future weather developments might be. The immediate local conditions are the ones that affect him most, and thus a background knowledge of weather generally, and of local conditions in particular, is important when making coastal passages.

Pressure systems
Most weather conditions are controlled by high or low pressure systems. These are indicated on the weather map as roughly concentric circles, the contours of which represent the gradients of pressure. These contour lines are termed *isobars*.

Weather patterns
All pressure systems move in a general west-east direction over Australia and thus some idea of the weather coming up can be gained by the pattern immediately to the west of your position. The speed of this movement varies and of course this creates problems in forecasting, but a close watch of the chart for a couple of days beforehand will give some indication of the speed at which the systems are moving.

A typical weather chart showing pattern of pressure systems.

High pressure weather.

High pressure system

This is the 'fine weather' system, usually bringing fine, warm
weather (or, at worst, light drizzle) with frosts, sometimes fogs
and light winds or sea breezes. The winds revolve around the
centre of the high anti-clockwise in the southern hemisphere.

Low pressure system

The 'bad weather' system. Low pressures almost always bring dirty weather often with heavy rain and strong winds. These are the systems that cause storms at sea and flooding along the coastlines. The winds follow the isobars around the low pressure cell in a clockwise direction (southern hemisphere).

Winds

Winds circulating around either high or low pressures increase as the steepness of the pressure gradient increases. Thus, the closer together the isobars on the weather chart, the stronger the winds.

Low pressure weather.

Most important part of weather forecasting for yachtsmen is predicting the winds.

Typical turbulent cloud of a cold front.

Fronts

These are turbulences caused by the mixing of hot and cold air. There are two frontal systems and, like the pressure systems, one is peaceful and quiet, the other stormy.

The cold front is a violent turbulence which can cause very strong winds, hail, rain and generally dangerous weather. The 'southerly buster' is a typical cold front where winds can reach 65 knots from a flat calm in almost seconds.

The warm front is the moderate system which usually brings only drizzle and overcast, mild conditions. Unlike the cold front, it takes some time to develop and is not one to worry small boats unduly.

Line squall

This is a form of cold front which has reached a very severe state. It gets its name from the roll of cloud that forms a line across the sky and is a condition to be avoided by small boats at all costs.

The unmistakable roll of cloud in a line squall.

Cyclones, hurricanes and typhoons

These are extremely deep depressions that have developed into tropical revolving storms. Their appearance on the chart is that of a tight whirlpool. Small boats, as a general rule, cannot survive this sort of storm condition and they must be avoided at all times.

Tropical storm seasons

Cyclones, hurricanes and typhoons are confined to tropical climates. Cyclones are the tropical revolving storms of the southern hemisphere encountered between November and March. Hurricanes are mostly encountered in the Caribbean waters and typhoons in South-East Asia. Their season is from July to October.

Sea breezes

The most common of local phenomena, sea breezes can be experienced along almost any coastline where the days are fairly hot. The sun, heating up the land masses inshore, cause convection currents with the warm air rising and drawing a cool

107

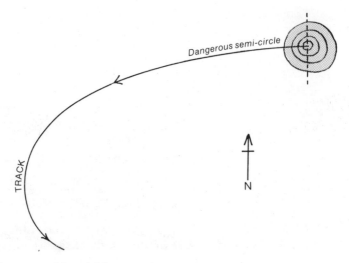

Cyclones travel in a fairly set path. The dangerous semicircle is the area directly in the path of the storm. Hurricanes curve northwards.

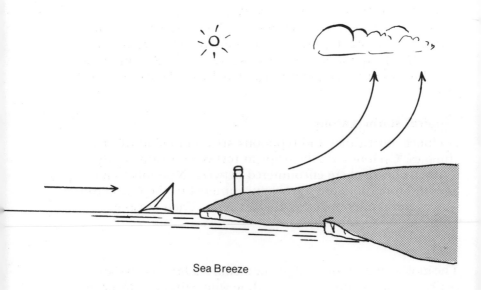

Sea Breeze

breeze off the sea to replace it. This sea breeze can pick up to 15
or 20 knots at times, the former being about the average.

Since it depends on sun for heating the land, the sea breeze is
almost always a fine weather condition and in fact it is the
superb summer phenomenon which brings excellent sailing
weather consistently throughout the season, except when it is
broken by a cold front or low pressure system.

Land breeze

During the night the land cools down quickly, while the sea
retains its heat. As a result, light convection currents set up over
the sea causing a cool breeze to be drawn off the land. However,
since the rising hot currents over the sea are much cooler than
those over the land during the day, the land breeze is a much
gentler breeze than the sea breeze.

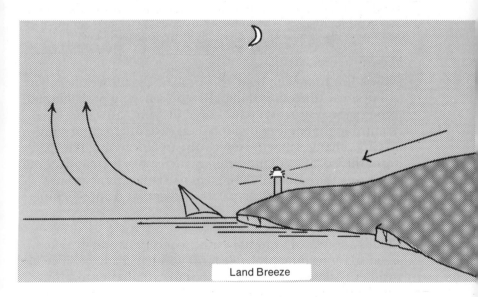

Land Breeze

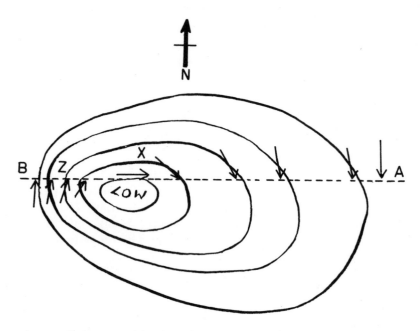

Assume the boat's position is at A. Then, as the low pressure system moves over to the eastwards, the weather will tend to deteriorate. Winds will back to the NW and then W as the centre of the depression passes over (X). They will continue to back to the SW and intensify in strength (Z) as the closer isobars of the trailing edge pass over. This is a southern hemisphere low.

Making a forecast

Draw a line from your boat's position across the weather chart in a westward direction. This will represent your probable path through the system as it passes over, moving eastwards. By examining the angle of the isobars at each intersection with this line, changes in wind direction can be forecast. The spacing of the isobars will indicate any increase or decrease in wind speed, and the nature of the system itself and any associated fronts will determine the type of weather that is approaching.

Clouds

Clouds are created by local weather conditions and therefore are ideal for reading probable local weather changes. Since the weather systems move roughly west to east, the approaching cloud will appear in the western sky. The following are the principal cloud patterns that indicate fairly certain weather conditions:

A. Fair weather cumulus. As their name denotes, harbingers of fine, summery conditions.

B. An approaching cold front indicating strong, turbulent conditions fairly close to hand.

C. Cirrostratus. High clouds which do not always bring the strong winds they indicate down to sea level.

D. Low scudding clouds which are usually rain-bearing and often associated with low pressure systems.

E. Cumulo nimbus or thunder clouds, often bringing turbulent conditions on hot days.

Other books by Jeff Toghill

The Boat Owner's Fitting-out Manual If you have just built or purchased a bare hull, this book will be all you need to grasp the right ways of doing your own fitting-out expertly and at minimum cost. It takes you step-by-step through the techniques of equipping your boat inside and out, giving you the theory, the right practice and the right material for a professional, yet money-saving job. 247 mm × 180 mm, 224 pages, 150 B&W photographs, 150 line drawings, cased and jacketed.

Small Boat Handling and Safety Anyone can jump into a power boat and race across a quiet waterway. But launching from a surf beach, riding out a heavy sea or crossing a bar are entirely different matters. The boat owner who takes pride in his boat and has taken the time to gain a thorough knowledge of her, how she responds in all situations and what her limitations are, will find himself able to meet difficult conditions and emergencies calmly and easily. 241 mm × 181 mm, 80 pages, 90 B&W photographs, limp.

The Yachtsman's Navigation Manual Covers every aspect of accurate navigation that might be needed by a yachtsman, whether making a ten kilometre coastal run or a ten thousand kilometre ocean voyage. The author moves from a consideration of basic equipment, the marine compass and charts to the details of laying off and plotting a course. There is a full discussion of the use of the sextant and all aspects of celestial navigation. 247 mm × 179 mm, 272 pages, fully illustrated with plates and line drawings.

Sailing for Beginners Starting with the basics, the author covers sails and rigging, how to get under way, sailing positions, boat handling, balancing, spinnakers, ropes, cordage and many other aspects of sailing including the problems of heavy weather and emergencies. 216 mm × 140 mm, 112 pages, illustrated, limp.

The Boat Owner's Maintenance Manual This book covers all aspects of the maintenance and repair of yachts, from sailing dinghys to keelers, and power craft from the small runabout to the large launch. Simplicity is the keynote throughout, with the emphasis on work which requires only a general knowledge of tools and paintbrush. The author deals with timber, fibreglass, aluminium and steel. 247 mm × 179 mm, 308 pages, fully illustrated with plates and line drawings, limp.